Hello and welcome!

Nachdem du neue Wörter in der Schule besprochen hast, kannst du die **New words** in diesem Buch als Vokabelheft benutzen.

Hello and welcome!
Ich bin der Wordmaster und helfe dir beim Wörterlernen.

Die **fett gedruckten** deutschen Wörter sind Lernwörter. Sie fehlen im englischen Satz, damit du sie eintragen kannst.

ction **1**

Meine Tipps

1 Die Reihenfolge der **New words** entspricht der Reihenfolge der neuen Wörter im Vocabulary deines Schülerbuches. Dort kannst du deine Lösungen überprüfen.

2 Wenn du mal nicht weiter weißt, kannst du auch im Vocabulary nachschauen.

3 Lern neue Wörter in einem Satz. So kann man sie sich besser merken.

4 Üb den neuen Wortschatz. Deck zum Beispiel mit einem Blatt Papier die englischen Sätze ab und versuch, die deutschen Sätze ins Englische zu übersetzen. Oder umgekehrt.

New words ▸ *p. 1*

Mein **Name** ist …	My <u>name</u> is …
Ich komme aus Deutschland.	<u>I'm from</u> Germany.
Ich gehe zur **Schule**.	I go to <u>school</u>.
Ich **lerne** Englisch.	I _____ English.
Unser **Lehrer** ist nett.	Our _____ is nice.

… das große R bedeutet Revision: Auf Deutsch Wiederholung. Hier übst du Vokabeln, die du bereits früher gelernt hast.

Hi! Ich bin Ken und gebe dir Tipps. Zum Beispiel …

Überhaupt: Es gibt neben **New words** viele lustige Übungen. Die Lösungen findest du im beigelegten Heftchen.

Introduction

New words ▸ *pp. 6 – 7*

Hast du schon die **Einführung** gelesen?	Have you read the _____ yet?
Wir haben viel Spaß in unserer **Jugend**gruppe.	We have lots of fun in our _____ group.
Dieser Fußballstar ist ein **National**held.	This football star is a _____ hero.
Welche Bands spielen auf dem **Fest**?	Which bands are playing at the _____ ?
Ist Wales ein Teil des **Vereinten Königreiches**?	Is Wales part of the _____ ?
Wir trafen Menschen **aus der ganzen Welt**.	We met people _____ .
Sie ist eine **geniale** Sängerin.	She's a _____ singer.
Welche **Art von** Musik magst du?	What _____ music do you like?
ein Konzert mit klassischer Musik	a _____ with _____ music
Hast du im **Workshop** viel gelernt?	Did you learn much at the _____ ?
Mein Freund **legt** jedes Wochenende **Platten auf**.	My friend _____ every weekend.
Aus welchem Land kommt das **Steeldrum**?	What country is the _____ from?
Man braucht **Stahl** um Brücken zu bauen.	You need _____ to build bridges.
Mein Vater spielt **Schlagzeug** und **Fiedel**.	My dad plays the _____ and the _____ .
Im **Norden** ist es meistens kälter.	It's usually colder in the _____ .

1 Lost words

Ergänze die Sätze mit den Wörtern im Feuerwerk.

1 ___In___ his youth grandpa was a very good swimmer.

2 What kind _____ music do your parents like?

3 People _____ all over Germany came to the concert.

4 What's the shortest way _____ the hostel?

5 There were three different bands _____ the gig.

6 _____ the way, where did you buy the steel drum?

7 B comes _____ C in the alphabet.

8 And D comes _____ C and E.

New words ▸ *pp. 8 – 9*

Wir verbrachten die Woche in einer **Herberge**.	We spent the week in a _____ .
Kannst du ein **Instrument** spielen?	Can you play an _____ ?
Wer ist der **Chef** hier?	Who's the _____ here?
Unsere Band hat jeden Monat einen **Auftritt**.	Our band does a _____ every month.
eine **Mischung** aus Jazz und klassischer Musik	a _____ of jazz and classical music
Wir spielen nicht nur **westliche** Musik.	We don't just play _____ music.

2 Verb forms

Ergänze die Tabelle der unregelmäßigen Verben.

1	keep	kept	kept	7	fly		
2		showed		8		read	
3	spend			9			thrown
4	hide			10			spoken
5		did		11		wrote	
6			taken	12	ride		

2 Crossword

Die Buchstabenrätsel helfen dir, die Lösungen zu finden. (↓ →)

(Crossword grid, with 2 across filled in: P R A C T I S E)

Across →

2 How long do you ★ the piano every day? (8)
4 TAURIG: You can find an instrument in these letters. (6)
5 In a ★, people sing and/or play music. (4)
7 – What can I do at the festival today?
   – Look at the ★ It has all the information. (9)
8 a famous singer, actor. etc. (4)
11 Nice to listen to: people sing it or play it on instruments (5)
12 I like this band best. It's my ★ band. (9)

Down ↓

1 MURD: You can find an instrument in these letters. (4)
2 This instrument has a black and white keyboard. (5)
3 Sue loves singing. She'd like to be a ★ in a band. (6)
6 great, super, very good (9)
7 What instrument do you ★? (4)
8 You sing it. (4)
9 Maybe one day I'll be rich and ★. (6)
10 You need one to get into the theatre or cinema. (6)

New words ▸ *pp. 10 – 11*

Warst du jemals in den **Vereinigten Staaten**?	Have you been to the _____ ?
Wie wär's mit Mittagessen? Ich bin **hungrig**!	_____ lunch? I'm _____ !
Nett, dich kennenzulernen.	_____
Eine halbe Stunde später kam er.	He came _____ later.
Er gab mir die **Hälfte** seiner Brote.	He gave me _____ of his sandwiches.
Lass uns **in Verbindung bleiben**.	Let's _____ .
Kannst du mir die Bilder **per E-Mail schicken**?	Can you _____ me the pictures?
Wird Tim auf der Party sein?– **Wart's ab**!	Will Tim be at the party? – _____
eine neue **Aufnahme** eines alten Liedes	a new _____ of an old song
Welches Bild **passt zu** welchem Wort?	Which picture _____ which word?
Kannst du **elektrische** Gitarre spielen?	Can you play the _____ guitar?
Ist das ein **Querflöte** oder eine **Blockflöte**?	Is that a _____ or a _____ ?
Ist ein **Saxophon** dasselbe wie eine **Trompete**?	Is a _____ the same as a _____ ?
Und wer spielt **Geige**?	And who plays the _____ ?

4 Last letter – first letter

*Der letzte Buchstabe von jedem Wort ist
gleichzeitig der erste des nächsten Wortes.*

1 Trommel
2 Mischung
3 elektrisch
4 Konzert
5 Trompete
6 Posaune
7 genug
8 Hälfte
9 Fiedel
10 Aufzug (AE)
11 Blockflöte

5 Word search

Finde im Gitter 9 Musikinstrumente.
Schreibe dann das englische Wort mit der deutschen Übersetzung auf. (↓ →)

M	V	I	O	L	I	N	V	R	W
S	G	X	P	I	A	N	O	R	M
R	U	X	Q	K	T	H	V	E	F
B	I	D	L	X	J	V	S	C	L
F	T	R	U	M	P	E	T	O	U
I	A	F	J	O	P	Q	H	R	T
D	R	L	I	D	R	U	M	D	E
D	Q	X	Y	A	H	C	F	E	T
L	Q	S	Q	A	L	O	M	R	N
E	S	A	X	O	P	H	O	N	E

violin – Geige

_____   _____

_____   _____

_____   _____

_____

6 Word groups

Trage die Wörter von der Wiese
in die richtigen Kletterseile ein.

clothes

jobs

places in town

animals

engineer   dress   deer   department store   fireman   frog   hedgehog   hospital   hostel
jacket   leisure centre   mole   paramedic   police station   policewoman   pyjamas
restaurant   shoes   skirt   squirrel   teacher   trousers   waiter   woodpecker

Unit 1

New words ▸ pp. 12–13

London ist die **Hauptstadt** von Großbritannien.　London is the _____ of Great Britain.

Die Aussicht vom **Riesenrad** ist toll.　The view from the _____ is fantastic.

Schau, dieses Auto hat nur drei **Räder**.　Look. This car has only got three _____ .

Wie heißt das deutsche **Parlament**?　What's the name of the German _____ ?

eine **Tondatei** kopieren　copy a _____

Kleider **aus zweiter Hand** sind oft billig.　_____ clothes are often cheap.

Hat England einen König oder eine **Königin**?　Has England got a king or a _____ ?

Kannst du dieses Lied für mich **aufnehmen**?　Can you _____ this song for me?

1 Word friends

*In jedem Haus gibt es drei Wörter bzw. Wortverbindungen,
die man direkt nach dem Verb auf der Fahne benutzen kann.
Unterstreiche sie.*

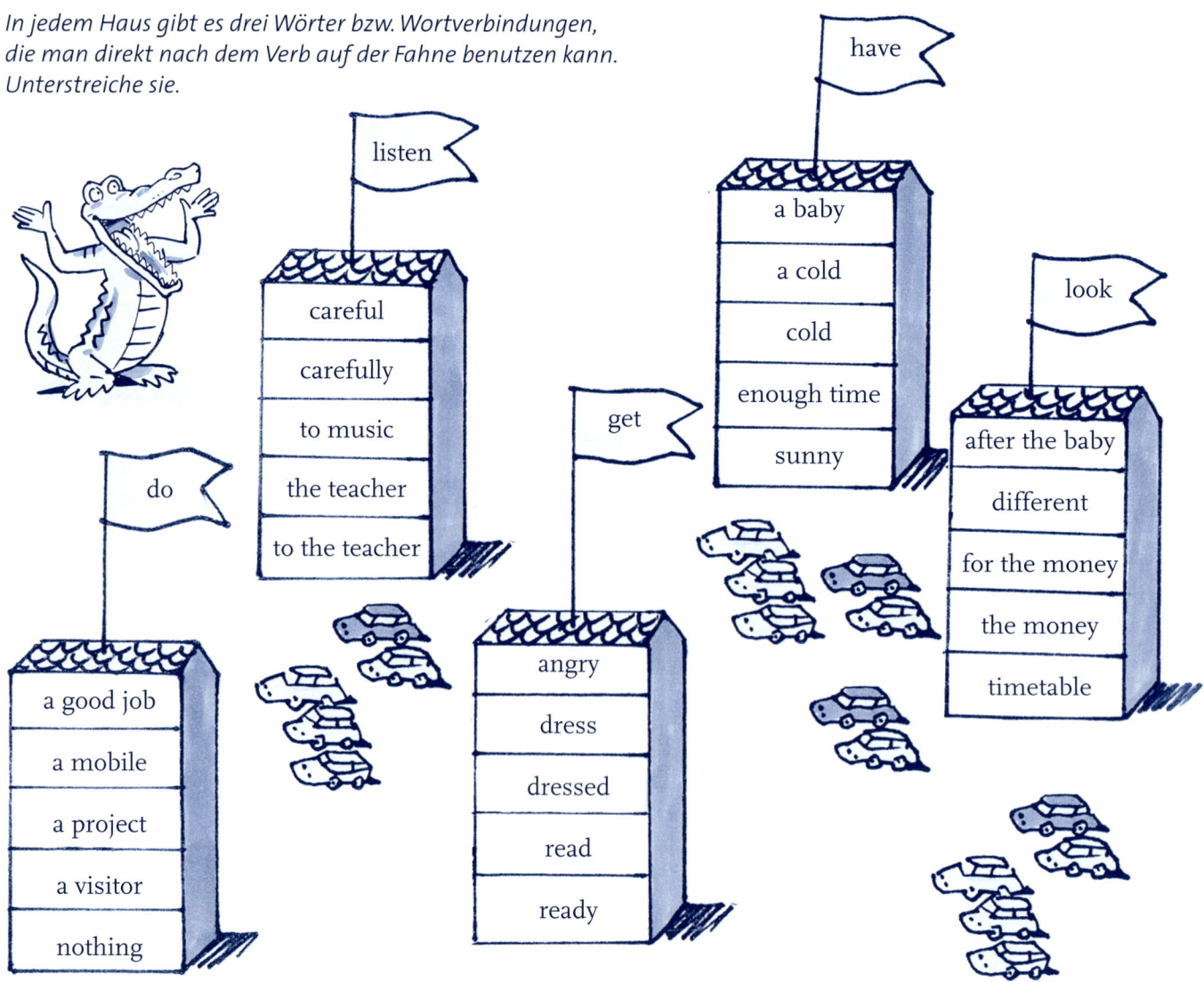

2 Classroom English

Welcher englische Satz ist korrekt – a, b oder c?

1   *Auf welcher Seite sind wir, bitte?*

     a   What for a page have we, please? ☐

     b   What side are we on, please? ☐

     c   What page are we on, please? ☐

2   *Ich habe meine Hausaufgaben vergessen.*

     a   I forgotten my homework. ☐

     b   I've forgotten my homework. ☐

     c   I have my homework forgotten. ☐

3   *Kannst du das bitte noch mal sagen?*

     a   Can you say that again, please? ☐

     b   Can you tell that again, please? ☐

     c   Can you that again say, please? ☐

4   *Kann ich es auf Deutsch sagen?*

     a   Can I say it on German? ☐

     b   Can I say it German? ☐

     c   Can I say it in German? ☐

3 Definitions

Vervollständige die Definitionen mit Wörtern aus den Mauersteinen. Trage die richtigen Wörter aus Kens Zeitung in die rechte Spalte ein.

wheels   palace
sights   concert
capital   queen

important	king	country	four	photos	
big	lots	king	~~move~~	places	live	woman

1   A car needs them to __m ove__ and usually has _____ of them.   *wheels*

2   the most _____ city in a _____   _____

3   interesting _____ in a city: tourists often take _____ of them   _____

4   an important _____ , often the wife of a _____   _____

5   a _____ building for a _____ or queen   _____

6   _____ music for _____ of people   _____

New words ▸ *pp. 14–15*

Drei **einfache Fahrkarten** kosten mehr	Three _____ cost more
... als eine **Tagesfahrkarte**.	... than a _____ .
Erwachsene müssen mehr als Kinder zahlen.	_____ have to pay more than children.
die Hauptstädte von **Mittel**europa besuchen	visit the capitals of _____ Europe
Fahren alle **Linien** in die Stadtmitte?	Do all _____ go to the city centre?
Ihr müsst am Piccadilly Circus **umsteigen**.	You have to _____ at Piccadilly Circus.
In London fahre ich immer mit der **U-Bahn**.	In London I always travel by _____ .
Hohe Gebäude haben meistens einen Fahrstuhl.	_____ buildings usually have a lift.

4 Spot the mistakes

In jedem Satz sind zwei Fehler. Unterstreiche und korrigiere sie.

1 London is the <u>kapital</u> off the United Kingdom.   *capital*   _____

2 The parlament building is one of London's famous saights.   _____   _____

3 We need two tikets for the unterground.   _____   _____

4 Take the Piccadilly linie for zentral London.   _____   _____

5 We'll have to chainge at Leicester Squar.   _____   _____

5 Word ladder

Gehe von unten nach oben, indem du bei jeder Sprosse einen Buchstaben veränderst.

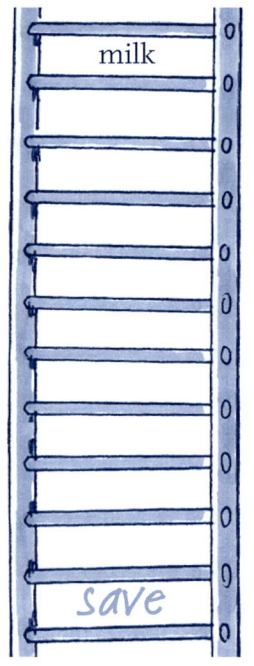

milk
save

Do you take ★ in your tea?

1.6 km = 1 ★.

This pen isn't ★. Is it yours?

good, OK

I don't understand this word in the first ★ of the text.

We live in the little house at the end of this ★.

the opposite of 'early'

What ★ is your birthday? – February 5th.

the opposite of 'love'

I'm staying in bed today because I ★ a cold.

Don't spend all your pocket money. Try and ★ some.

6 More about ... London Underground

Vervollständige den Text mit den Wörtern aus der Box.

~~also~~ although and
because before ground
more only too when

London Underground is the oldest underground railway in the world. People *also* (1) call it the 'Tube'

_____ (2) the tunnels look like *tubes. The first line opened in 1863. It was _____ (3) six

kilometres long. The first electric trains came in 1890; _____ (4) that, there were *steam trains.

Today there are 12 lines _____ (5) 275 stations. Together all the lines are 408 kilometres long,

but only 185 kilometres are under the _____ (6). Outside the city centre, the lines run over ground

_____ (7). In 1863, _____ (8) the Underground opened, 41,000 people travelled on the first

day. Today _____ (9) than 3 million people use the Tube every day. _____ (10) it's more

expensive than going by bus, it's the fastest way to travel around London.

tube = Röhre; steam train = Dampfzug

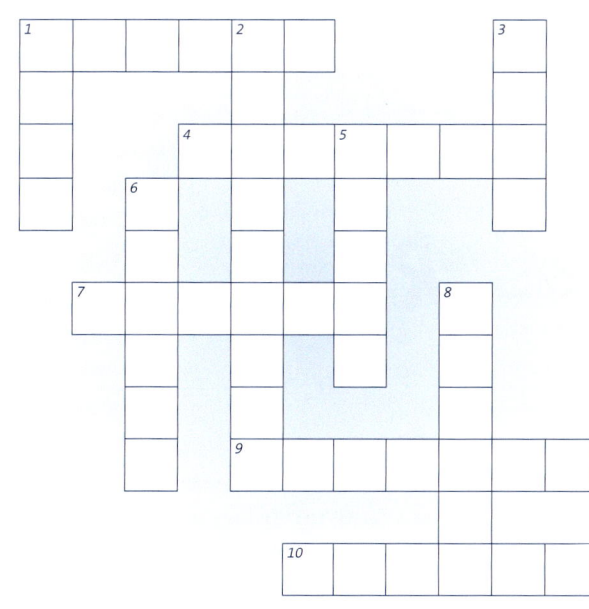

7 Crossword: places in a city

Die Buchstabenrätsel helfen dir, die Lösungen zu finden. (↓ →)

Across
1 CAPELA: Kings and queens live here. (6)
4 SIONTAT: Trains arrive and leave from here. (7)
7 BIEGDR: This helps you to cross a river. (6)
9 RIBALRY: You can find lots of books here. (7)
10 EUUMMS: Go to this place to see old and interesting things. (6)

Down
1 KRAP: Go here to walk, relax or play. (4)
2 DALERCATH: a very important church (9)
3 NALE: a kind of road (4)
5 TWREO: a high building (5)
6 SICCUR: a round place with buildings around it (6)
8 SERQUA: a place with buildings on four sides (6)

New words ▸ p. 16

Ich habe ihn nur **einmal** gesehen	I only saw him _____
... oder war es **zweimal**?	... or was it _____ ?
Ich komme drei Mal **pro** Woche hierher.	I come here three times _____ week.
Möchtest du ein **Curry**gericht oder eine Pizza?	Would you like _____ or a Pizza?
Für mich ist das Essen zu **scharf gewürzt**.	The food is too _____ for me.
Ich möchte etwas **Mildes** probieren.	I'd like to try something _____ .
Mein Lieblings**gericht** ist Pommes und Bratwurst.	My favourite _____ is chips and sausage.

8 Hidden words

Ergänze die Wortgruppen, indem du Wörter mit Buchstaben des Wortes „parliament" bildest.

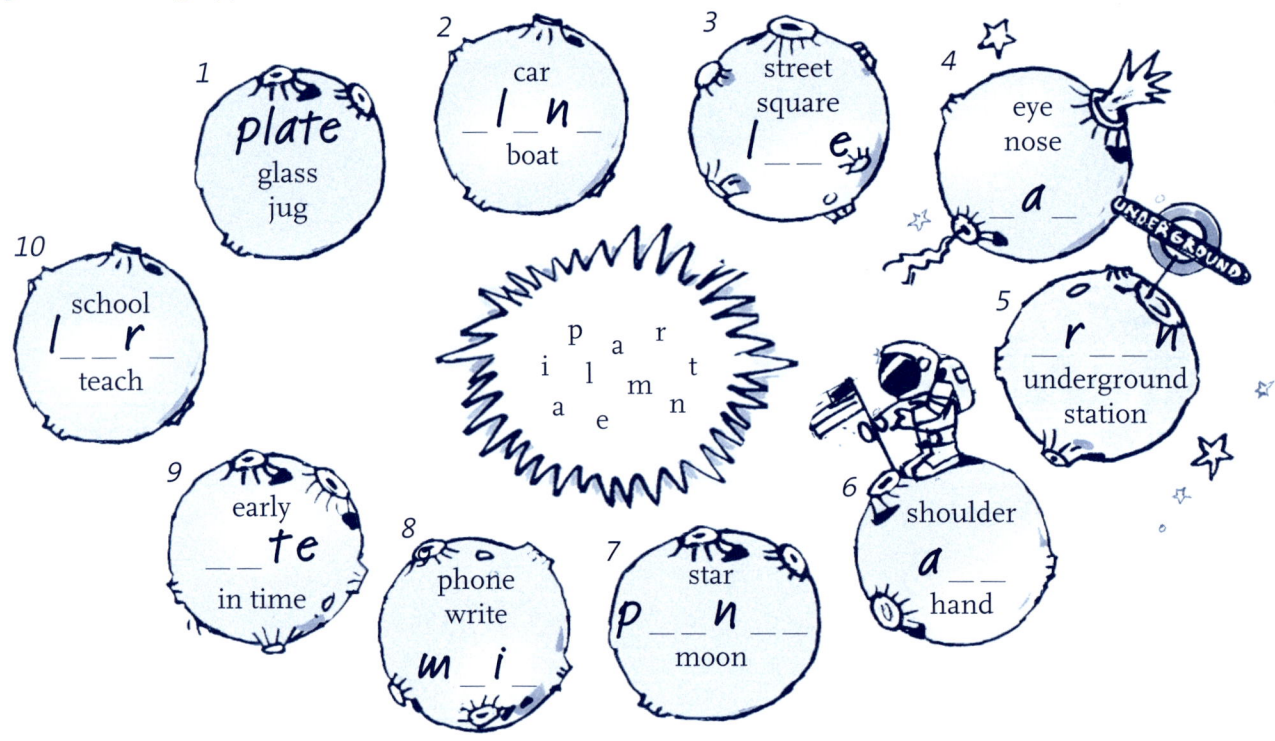

1 plate / glass / jug
2 car / _ l _ n _ / boat
3 street / square / l _ _ _ e
4 eye / nose / _ _ a _
5 r / _ _ _ _ n / underground station
6 shoulder / a _ _ _ / hand
7 star / P _ _ _ n _ _ / moon
8 phone / write / m _ i _
9 early / _ _ te / in time
10 school / l _ _ r _ / teach

9 Word families

Finde die passenden Verben zu den angegebenen Nomen.

1 explanation – *explain*
2 winner – _____
3 smile – _____
4 flight – _____

5 actor – _____
6 laughter – _____
7 building – _____
8 description – _____

9 rehearsal – _____
10 glue – _____
11 movement – _____
12 explorer – _____

10 Word building

Verbinde ein Wort aus der Liste mit einem Wort auf den Noten. Trage die deutsche Übersetzung ein.

centre end lessons boots ball room work bell chair star file tree

1 dancing *lessons* *Tanzstunden* _____

2 family_____ _____

3 sports_____ _____

4 sound_____ _____

5 football_____ _____

6 film_____ _____

7 door*bell*_____ _____

8 class_____ _____

9 home_____ _____

10 wheel_____ _____

11 foot_____ _____

12 week_____ _____

11 Odd word out

Ein Wort passt nicht. Finde und unterstreiche es.

1 cathedral – palace – museum – adult

2 giraffe – budgie – hippo – rhino

3 recorder – CD player – trumpet – flute

4 trendy – sweet – mild – spicy

5 potato – carrot – dish – banana

6 planet – sun – ball – moon

12 The best word

Finde das Wort in der Strickleiter, das am besten in die Lücke passt.

1 Why are you so _____ with me? I haven't done anything wrong.

2 Paul is so _____ . He even finds it hard to say hello to people.

3 Kim felt very _____ when she won the first prize.

4 Rob looked _____ . He didn't understand the joke.

5 Don't be _____ . The dog really isn't dangerous.

6 We were a bit _____ before the test, but it was actually OK.

angry	nervous
nice	shy
alone	puzzled
happy	shy
angry	proud
sad	sorry
happy	puzzled
proud	scared
alone	scared
proud	sorry
happy	nice
nervous	sorry

New words ▸ pp. 20–25

die **Beförderung** zwischen Bahnhof und Hotel

_____ between station and hotel

ein Tunnel unter dem **Erdboden**

a tunnel under the _____

Ich will einen Englisch**kurs** in England machen.

I want do to an English _____ in England.

Papa mag viel **Butter** auf dem Brot.

Dad likes lots of _____ on his bread.

Wir brauchen Obst und **Gemüse**.

We need fruit and _____ .

Unser **Fleischer** macht die besten Würstchen.

Our _____ makes the best sausages.

Diese **Bäckerei** macht leckeres Brot.

This _____ makes delicious bread.

Wir sind bloß eine normale **Alltags**familie.

We're just a normal _____ family.

Warum hast du deine **Reise unterbrochen**?

Why did you _____ your _____ ?

die **Fahrt** zur Schule

the _____ to school

War diese **Durchsage** für unseren Zug?

Was that _____ for our train?

13 Word search

*Finde im Rätsel 16 deutsche Begriffe zum Thema Verkehr.
Schreibe dann das deutsche Wort und die englische
Übersetzung auf. (↓ →)*

U	L	F	F	A	H	R	P	L	A	N	S
M	A	L	L	S	Z	X	A	T	B	F	T
S	S	U	U	J	U	A	U	A	A	A	R
T	T	G	G	J	G	B	S	X	H	E	A
E	W	S	Z	B	U	S	S	I	N	H	S
I	A	T	E	A	U	P	T	N	S	R	S
G	G	E	U	U	I	Y	E	C	T	E	E
E	E	I	G	T	C	M	I	C	E	Z	N
N	N	G	R	O	J	B	G	W	I	F	B
F	L	U	G	H	A	F	E	N	G	O	A
C	V	C	Q	B	A	H	N	H	O	F	H
E	F	E	I	N	S	T	E	I	G	E	N

Fahrplan – timetable

_____

_____

_____

_____

_____

_____

_____

_____

_____

_____

_____

New words ▶ pp. 26–27

Es ist sicherer, einen Fahrrad**helm** zu tragen.   It's safer to wear a bike _____ .

Was steht auf dem **Schild**?   What does the _____ say?

Ruf die Polizei, wenn du in **Gefahr** bist.   Call the police if you're in _____ .

Vor einem Flug bin ich immer **aufgeregt**.   I'm always _____ before a flight.

Drück auf den **Knopf** und die Tür wird aufgehen.   Push the _____ and the door will open.

Kannst du bitte einen **Moment** warten?   Can you wait a _____ please?

Dieser Plan ist nicht sehr **realistisch**.   This plan isn't very _____ .

Er ist **freundlich** und lächelt immer.   He's _____ and always smiles.

Er war **schockiert** über die schlechte Nachricht.   He was _____ about the bad news.

Zieh bitte den **Stecker** nicht heraus.   Please don't pull out the _____ .

14 The fourth word

Welches Wort fehlt hier?

1 bread – food   trumpet – *instrument*   6 bad – good   wrong – _____

2 man – woman   king – _____   7 under 18 – child   over 18 – _____

3 east – west   north – _____   8 horse – legs   car – _____

4 US – United States   UK – _____   9 shoe – foot   helmet – _____

5 danger – dangerous   centre – _____   10 one time – once   two times – _____

15 Opposites

Trage die Gegenteile der fett gedruckten Wörter in die Lücken ein.

1 an **international** / a *national* festival   8 Are you planning to **arrive** / _____ early?

2 Do you like **mild** / _____ dishes?   9 Only **poor** / _____ people live in this street.

3 This room is very **dirty** / _____ .   10 Is the supermarket **open** / _____ ?

4 Turn **left** / _____ at the next corner.   11 buy a **return** / _____ ticket

5 whisper **quietly** / shout _____   12 She has lots of **enemies** / _____

6 a **strong** / _____ person   13 **noisy** / _____ neighbours

7 It's **possible** / _____ to get there by bus.   14 **happy** / _____ faces

New words ▸ *pp. 28–29*

ein **Lichtblitz** am Himmel	a _____ in the sky
Die Geschichte hatte ein unglückliches **Ende**.	The story had an unhappy _____ .
Wie komme ich voran?	_____ ?
Wir wohnen in einer ruhigen **Gegend**.	We live in a quiet _____ .
Ja, dies ist eine **Tatsache**.	Yes, this is a _____ .

16 Pronunciation

Ordne die Wörter aus der Box der richtigen Aussprachegruppe zu.

Wenn ihr mal Probleme mit der Aussprache habt, hilft die Lautschrift im Dictionary!

already   beach   bread   breakfast   cheap   clean
clear   dead   dear   disappear   ear   eastbound
head   idea   leave   near   ready   tea

e	iː	ɪə
already	clean	dear
_____	_____	_____
_____	_____	_____
_____	_____	_____
_____	_____	_____
_____	_____	_____

17 One or two letters?

Trage die fehlenden Buchstaben ein:
d *oder* **dd**, **f** *oder* **ff**, **n** *oder* **nn**.

d dd   fi____le, mi____le , stu____ent, hi____en, rea____y, mo____el

f ff   a____raid, gira____e, tra____ic, o____ten, di____icult, le____t

n nn   a____other, begi____ing, di____er, tu____el, e____emy, pe____cil

l l   a____phabet, a____ways, bri____iant, rea____istic, a____one, pu____over

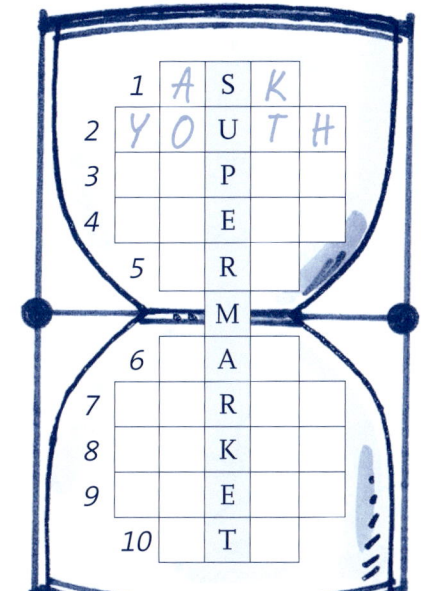

18 Hour glasses

Übersetze die Wörter und trage sie in die passende Sanduhr ein.

	1	A	S	K		
2	Y	O		T	H	
3			P			
4			E			
	5		R			
			M			
6			A			
7			R			
8			K			
9			E			
	10		T			

1 fragen – Eis

2 Jugend – ungefähr

3 Zeitung - Römer/-in

4 Entschuldigung – glücklich

5 Tasche – Arm

6 Mülltonne – Mütze

7 schmutzig – Aufsatz

8 Torten – Zahn

9 Geld – jubeln

10 aß – benutzen

	1	I	C	E		
2						
3						
4						
	5					
6						
7						
8						
9						
	10					

Die geheime Wort in der rechten Sanduhr heißt: Englisch _____

Deutsch _____

19 Picture puzzle

Vergleiche die beiden Bilder miteinander. Welche 8 Gegenstände fehlen auf dem rechten Bild?

a purse _____   _____

_____   _____

_____   _____

_____   _____

Unit 2

New words ▸ *p. 30*

eine Stadt an der Süd**küste** von England	a town on the south _____ of England
Um die Insel herum liegen viele **Felsen**.	There are lots of _____ around the island.
Wir brauchen etwas **Öl** für unseren Salat.	We need some _____ for our salad.
Mein Vater arbeitet auf einer **Bohrinsel**.	My father works on an _____ .

1 Word friends

Welche Wörter aus den Kieselsteinen passen in die Lücken?

listen   wait   become   eat   do   know   speak   catch   read   keep

1 *eat*____ meat / a big lunch /too much

2 _____ for a bus / for 10 minutes / outside

3 _____ a ball / a thief / the bank robbers

4 _____ a good book /and write / a brochure

5 _____ two languages / more slowly / to me

6 _____ to the radio / for the doorbell

7 _____ all the answers / lots of people

8 _____ crosswords / your homework / judo

9 _____ a teacher / tired / very excited

10 _____ in touch / the window open

2 Classroom English

Welcher englische Satz ist korrekt – a, b oder c?

1   Was meinst du?

a What mean you? ☐

b What do you think? ☐

c What think you? ☐

2   Wie fandest du die Geschichte?

a Where did you find the story? ☐

b Did you find the story? ☐

c Did you like the story? ☐

3   Ich finde, Alex hat recht.

a I think Alex is right. ☐

b I think Alex has right. ☐

c I think Alex had right. ☐

New words ► *p. 32*

Meine Eltern mögen keine **elektronische** Musik.	My parents don't like _____ music.
die neuen **Medien** wie das Internet oder E-Mail	the new _____ like the internet or e-mail
Schick mir eine **SMS**.	Send me a _____ .
Ich habe eine wichtige **Nachricht** für dich.	I've got an important _____ for you.
Kannst du mir die Nummer **per SMS schicken**?	Can you _____ me the number?
Rob und ich sind immer gute **Kumpel** gewesen.	Rob and I have always been good _____ .
Zeit haben **im Internet** zu **surfen**	have time to _____
Darf man diese Datei **herunterladen**?	Is it OK to _____ this file?
Wir können diese zwei Lieder **mischen**.	We can _____ these two songs.
Magst du diese **Mischung** aus Rock und Pop?	Do you like this _____ of pop and rock?
Ich habe einen neuen **Klingelton** für mein Handy.	I've got a new _____ for my mobile.

3 The fourth word

Welches Wort fehlt hier?

1	apple – fruit	onion – _____	6	up – down	top – _____
2	good – bad	clever – _____	7	ridden – ride	forgotten – _____
3	meat – butcher's	bread – _____	8	heard – hear	taught – _____
4	build – building	fly – _____	9	husband – husbands	wife – _____
5	cow – beef	pig – _____	10	clinic – doctor	farm – _____

4 Odd word out

Unterstreiche das Wort, das nicht passt.

1 car – farm – bus – bike

2 mountain – lake – farmer – coast

3 danger – farmer – butcher – waiter

4 onion – mushroom – bacon – pea

5 lorry – ferry – boat – ship

6 tired – hungry – cold – station

7 first – second – three – fourth

8 first – west – north – south

9 mail – write – wait – phone

10 surf – mate – download – text

11 meat – fruit – salad – oil rig

12 button – shirt – jeans – jacket

New words ▸ *p. 33*

Wie lange **dauert** der Flug nach Berlin?	How long does the flight to Berlin _____ ?
Ich kann dich am Flughafen **abholen**.	I can _____ you _____ at the airport.
Die **Ankunft**szeit ist jeden Tag dieselbe.	The _____ time is the same every day.
Kannst du mir die **Abfahrt**szeit sagen?	Can you tell me the _____ time?
Er kam früh und blieb **bis** 13 Uhr.	He came early and stayed _____ 1 pm.
Es tut mir leid – ich werde nicht kommen **können**.	I'm sorry – I won't _____ to come.

5 Words with different meanings

Finde in der Liste die passenden Wörter zu den Paaren 1–7.
Trage sie ein und unterstreiche die deutschen Entsprechungen.

3
a) die <u>An</u>kunftszeit im Fahrplan suchen
b) der Stundenplan für das neue Schuljahr

2
a) Vergiss nicht das Wechselgeld.
b) Wo müssen wir umsteigen?

1
a) Ist er <u>ledig</u> oder verheiratet?
b) eine <u>einfache</u> Fahrkarte kaufen

single

5
a) Papa hört gern Rockmusik.
b) Lass uns bis zu diesem Fels schwimmen.

4
a) Du darfst nicht soviel Geld ausgeben!
b) Wir verbringen unseren Sommerurlaub immer am Meer.

change
rock
timetable
single
spend
walk

6
a) Lass uns zu Fuß gehen!
b) einen Spaziergang machen

6 Last letter – first letter

Der letzte Buchstabe von jedem Wort ist
gleichzeitig der erste des nächsten Wortes.

1 Fahrplan
2 aufgeregt
3 Abfahrt
4 Elefant
5 dauern/(Zeit) brauchen
6 Aufzug
7 Fels
8 Schlüssel
9 du/ihr/dir/euch
10 bis
11 zum Glück
12 schon

7 Word groups

Übersetze die deutschen Wörter auf den Zetteln ins Englische und füge sie in die richtige Wortgruppe ein.

farm animals	media	transport
chicken		

Handy Schaf Lamm
Zeitung Abfahrt Bahnhof
Truthahn Huhn
Kuh
Pferd Radio Zeitschrift
Fernsehen Ankunft
U-Bahn Fahrplan
Bushaltestelle Tondatei

8 Spot the mistakes

In jedem Satz sind zwei Fehler. Unterstreiche und korrigiere sie. Es gibt Rechtschreib- und grammatische Fehler.

1 Hoy is one of the biger Orkney ilands.   *bigger* _____   _____

2 Katrina kieps in touch with people all over the werld.   _____   _____

3 She have a mobil, so she often texts her friends.   _____   _____

4 She also write e-mails once or twice a weak.   _____   _____

5 She sometimes downloads musik from a webseite.   _____   _____

6 Last weekend she taked lots of fotos at the ceilidh.   _____   _____

9 Crossword

Across
1 You hear this when someone calls you on your mobile. (8)
4 where the sea meets land (5)
6 very big (4)
8 two times (5)
9 a word for television, radio, newpapers, etc. (5)
10 You need this for a car – and you use it to make a salad. (3)

Down
1 Something very hard – you find them in the mountains or at the coast. (4)
2 two times – twice / one time – ★ (4)
3 another word for 'friend' (4)
5 opposite of 'departure' (4)
7 The film was boring, so we didn't stay ★ the end. (5)
9 If the juice is too sweet, ★ it with water. (5)

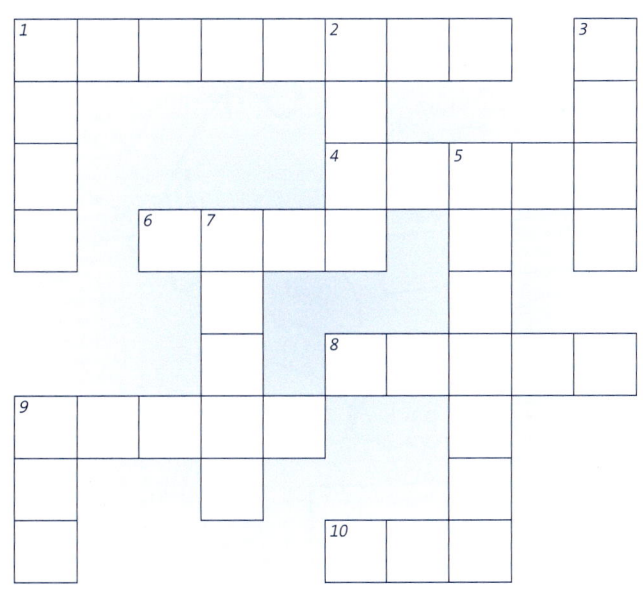

New words ▸ *pp. 34–35*

modische T-Shirts kaufen	buy some _____ t-shirts
Ich mag ihn – er ist ein freundlicher **Typ**.	I like him – he's a friendly _____ .
Wir mussten einen großen **Rucksack** packen.	We had to pack a big _____ .
Ich kann nicht weggehen – ich **erwarte** Besucher.	Ican't got out – I'm _____ visitors.
Ich bin **gekränkt**, weil du unhöflich zu mir warst.	I'm _____ because you were rude to me.
Es **kränkt** mich, wenn du unhöflich bist.	It _____ me when you're rude.
Könntest du bitte das Licht **einschalten?**	Could you _____ the light, please?
Schalt das Radio **aus**, wenn du nicht hörst.	_____ the radio _____ if you aren't listening.
Wir sind **froh**, dass ihr hier seid.	We are _____ , that you are here.
die **Schönheit** der Berge Schottlands	the _____ of Scotland's mountains
Er **hat** mir wieder **Schimpfwörter nachgerufen.**	He _____ me _____ again.
Ich **würde** mich auf einer Insel alleine fühlen.	I _____ feel alone on an island.
Leider gibt's an jeder Schule einen **Schultyrannen**.	I'm afraid there's a _____ at every school.
Wie spät ist es? Es ist **genau** sechs Uhr.	What's the time? It's _____ six o'clock.
Ich habe ein Problem, also brauche ich deinen **Rat**.	I have a problem, so I need your _____ .

10 Word pairs

Welche Wörter passen zusammen?

ball
course
helmet
menu
message
recorder
rucksack
sound file

download · send · wear · message · pack · do · read · play · catch

11 Scrambled words: school

Löse die Buchstabenrätsel, um Wörter zu finden, die mit Schule zusammenhängen.
Trage die deutschen Übersetzungen ein. Die markierten Buchstaben ergeben das „geheime Wort".

1 Teal Bit Em   T I M E T A B L E   *Stundenplan*

2 Trace Eh –   _ _ _ _ _ _   _____

3 Cam Tassel   _ _ _ _ _ _ _   _____

4 Hay Idols –   _ _ _ _ _ _ _   _____

5 Bad Or   _ _ _ _ _   _____

6 Sic Enec   _ _ _ _ _ _   _____

7 Carom Loss   _ _ _ _ _ _ _ _   _____

12 The best word

Finde das Wort in der Strickleiter, das am besten in die Lücke passt.

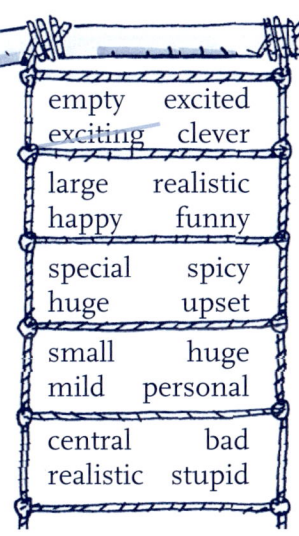

empty	excited
exciting	clever
large	realistic
happy	funny
special	spicy
huge	upset
small	huge
mild	personal
central	bad
realistic	stupid

1 Here's some _exciting_ news. Mum's going to have another baby!

2 Open a window please. There's a _____ smell in the room.

3 Kim was very _____ because nobody came to visit her.

4 They live in a _____ house with 17 bedrooms.

5 Fantastic! That's a very _____ plan.

13 Making phrases

Vervollständige die Audrücke mit dem Verb vom richtigen Zettel.

1 _take_ a photo of the cows in the field

2 _____ a text message to a friend

3 _____ the arrival times in the timetable

4 _____ all the hungry farm animals

5 _____ the train at the next station

6 _____ your mum on your mobile

take

check   get off   phone

send   feed

New words ▶ *pp. 38–41*

Kannst du meinen Namen **erraten**?	Can you _____ my name?
allgemeine und besondere Informationen	_____ and special information
Es ist **persönlich**. Ich möchte nicht darüber reden.	It's _____ . I don't want to talk about it.
Bist du sicher, ob diese **Aussage** korrekt ist?	Are you sure if this _____ is correct?
Geld für einen neuen **Monitor** sparen	save money for a new _____
Drück auf den Knopf, um das Radio einzuschalten.	_____ the button to turn on the radio.
Vergiss nicht, die Haustür **abzuschließen**.	Don't forget to _____ the front door.
Schließ bitte das Auto **auf** – ich will einsteigen.	Please _____ the car – I want to get in.

14 Word search: town and country

Im Rätsel sind 18 „town and country"-Wörter versteckt.
Finde sie und übersetze sie ins Deutsche. (↓ →)

O	I	A	J	F	I	E	L	D	S	F	K
S	G	R	O	A	D	B	U	I	T	X	B
Q	L	F	F	H	A	R	B	O	U	R	R
U	A	A	M	O	U	N	T	A	I	N	I
A	K	R	K	V	G	U	S	Y	Z	T	D
R	E	M	H	I	L	L	M	C	I	O	G
E	S	O	B	B	J	P	Y	A	S	W	E
O	E	S	T	A	T	I	O	N	L	E	S
C	A	S	T	L	E	E	M	A	A	R	K
B	B	E	A	C	H	V	V	L	N	Q	N
D	A	X	C	O	A	S	T	O	D	X	O
C	T	H	R	I	V	E	R	Q	I	B	Q

field _____ Feld, Acker

_____ _____

_____ _____

_____ _____

_____ _____

_____ _____

_____ _____

_____ _____

_____ _____

_____ _____

_____ _____

_____ _____

_____ _____

_____ _____

_____ _____

_____ _____

_____ my name?

15 More about ... Orkney

Vervollständige den Text mit Wörtern vom Ticket.

Orkney is a group of <u>islands</u> (1) ten miles from the Scottish coast. Today, about

20,000 people live _____ (2) 17 of the 70 islands. Most – about 15,000 – live on the

_____ (3) island, Mainland. Between five _____ (4) 550 people live on the

other islands. Hoy, the second largest island, has just under 300 people.

  Orkney hasn't got many people, _____ (5) it has lots of schools – 21 for about 3,300

VisitOrkney
www.visitorkney.com

students. Some of the schools are very small – four of them have

_____ (6) ten students.

When people travel from one island to _____ (7) they go by

ferry, or fly between the bigger islands. The shortest flight is

_____ (8) Westray and Papa Westray – it _____ (9)

only two minutes.

Orkney is great _____ (10) holidays. If you go there, you can

stay on a farm and learn how to _____ (11) cheese, enjoy the

clean air and beautiful beaches and find out more about the 5,500

year _____ (12) of the people on the islands.

Ticket words:
another
between
biggest
but
and
for
history
islands
make
on
takes
under

16 Lost words

Die fehlenden Wörter stecken im Maul des Hais.
Finde sie und ergänze die Sätze.

1 The water here can be dangerous, so it's <u>unsafe</u> to go swimming.

2 It's _____ to eat fruit and vegetables every day.

3 Jane's room is always in a mess – she's so _____ !

4 I think it's _____ if you don't do any sport.

5 Sue never laughs or smiles. She can't be a very _____ person.

6 Tim never says hello to anyone. Why is he so _____ ?

7 Which of you knows the _____ answer?

8 Jo was very _____ when he lost his favourite earring.

9 I'm _____ to hear that you aren't feeling well.

happy
healthy
unsafe
untidy
unhealthy
unfriendly
upset
right
sorry

New words ▸ *pp. 44–47*

Kannst du bitte das **Licht** einschalten?	Can you turn on the _____ , please?
Möchtest du **eine Tasse** Tee?	Would you like a _____ ?
Die **Schulversammlung** begann um 8.50.	_____ started at 8.50.
Der **Schulleiter** machte eine Ankündigung.	The _____ made an announcement.
Dies sind großartige **Neuigkeiten**.	That's great _____ !
Ein Geschenk! Das ist eine nette **Überraschung**!	A present! That's a nice _____ !
Er rannte schnell **über** die Straße.	He ran quickly _____ the road.
Dieser **Anorak** ist schön warm.	This _____ is nice and warm.
Ich denke, ich werde ein **Mikrofon** brauchen.	I think I'll need a _____ .
Der Englischtest ist **gut verlaufen**.	The English test _____ .
Könnt ihr die Kirchen**glocken** hören?	Can you hear the church _____ ?
Das Schaf Dolly war ein berühmter **Klon**.	The sheep Dolly was a famous _____ .
Ist er **neidisch auf** meinen neuen Computer?	Is he _____ my new computer?
Die meisten Dörfer haben eine **Gemeindehalle**.	Most villages have a _____ .
Wie kann ich dieses Wort **übersetzen**?	How can I _____ this word?
Die ist keine gute **Übersetzung**.	This isn't a good _____ .
ein Wort im Wörterbuch **nachschlagen**	_____ a word in the dictionary
die **Bedeutung** eines Wortes verstehen	_____ the meaning of a word

17 Opposites

Trage die Gegenteile der fett gedruckten Wörter in die Lücken ein.

1 a **boring** / an _____ film

2 wear a **new** / an _____ anorak

3 look **happy** / _____

4 Turn **left** / _____ at the next corner.

5 buy some **summer** / _____ clothes

6 a film for kids **under** / _____ 12

7 Let's play **inside** / _____ .

8 in the **morning** / _____

9 I **love** / _____ fish and chips.

10 He's a **friendly** / an _____ man.

11 There's **somebody** / _____ here.

12 **ask** / _____ questions

18 Vocabulary network

Vervollständige das Wörternetz.
Die Verben, die auf den Zetteln
fehlen, bringt der Geier.
Die anderen Wörter findest du
im Sand.

Unit 3

New words ▸ pp. 52–53

Hast du wirklich Karten für das **Endspiel**?

Have you really got tickets for the _____ ?

Leider wird dies sein **letztes** Spiel sein.

I'm afraid this will be his _____ game.

Er gewann das **Halbfinale**, verlor aber das Endspiel.

He won the _____ , but lost the final.

eine **Trainingseinheit** verpassen

miss a _____

den **Steckbrief** einer Person anschauen

look at a person's _____

Er verließ die Schule im **Alter** von 18.

He left school at the _____ of 18.

Welches **Geschlecht** hat das neue Baby?

What _____ is the new baby?

Mädchen sind **weiblich** und

Girls are _____ and

... Jungen sind **männlich**.

boys are _____ .

Der Bahnhof ist ein guter **Standort** für den Laden.

The station's a good _____ for the shop.

1 Words in pictures

a) Trage die angezeigten Körperteile ein.

1 _face_

2 _____

3 _____

4 _____

5 _____

6 _____

7 _____

8 _____

9 _____

b) Unterstreiche die beiden Wörter, die am besten zu den fettgedruckten Wörtern passen.

1 a broken / pretty / round **face**

2 blue / bright / loud **eyes**

3 a long / small / tidy **nose**

4 my left / medium / right **ear**

5 broken / careful / white **teeth**

6 grey / slow / tidy **hair**

7 a big / early / loud **mouth**

8 cheap / clean / strong **hands**

2 Hidden words

Ergänze die Wortgruppen, indem du Wörter mit Buchstaben der Wörter „training session" bildest.

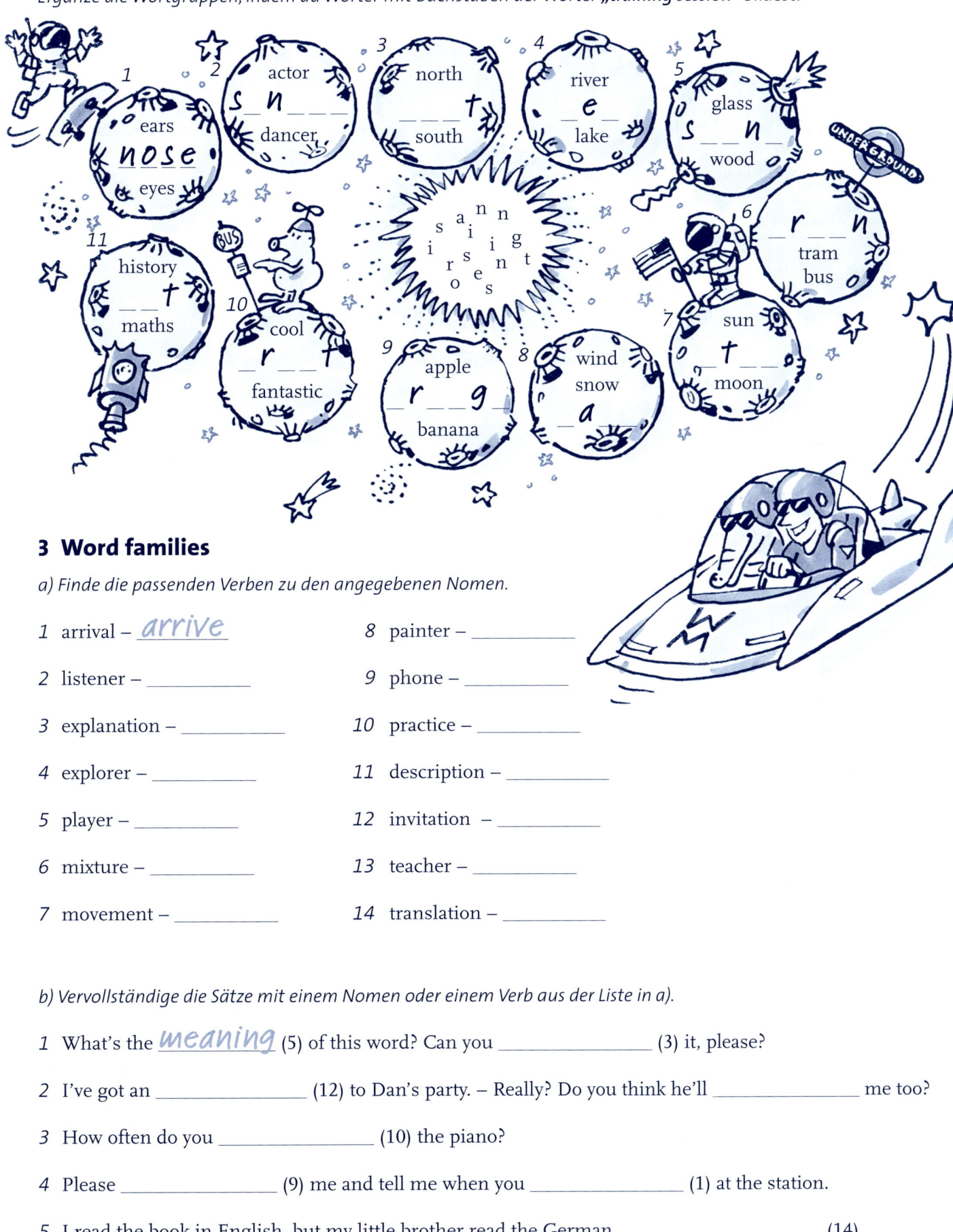

3 Word families

a) Finde die passenden Verben zu den angegebenen Nomen.

1 arrival – *arrive*

2 listener – _____

3 explanation – _____

4 explorer – _____

5 player – _____

6 mixture – _____

7 movement – _____

8 painter – _____

9 phone – _____

10 practice – _____

11 description – _____

12 invitation – _____

13 teacher – _____

14 translation – _____

b) Vervollständige die Sätze mit einem Nomen oder einem Verb aus der Liste in a).

1 What's the *meaning* (5) of this word? Can you _____ (3) it, please?

2 I've got an _____ (12) to Dan's party. – Really? Do you think he'll _____ me too?

3 How often do you _____ (10) the piano?

4 Please _____ (9) me and tell me when you _____ (1) at the station.

5 I read the book in English, but my little brother read the German _____ (14).

New words ▶ pp. 54–55

Klopfe, bevor du den Raum **betrittst**!	Knock before you _____ the room!
ein deutscher **Austauschschüler** in England	a German _____ in England
Hungrig? – Nein, ich habe keinen **Appetit**.	Hungry? – No, I've got no _____ .
Es ist schon 11 Uhr. Ich **wette**, wir sind zu spät.	It's already eleven o'clock. I _____ we're late.
Magst du wirklich **Leber** mit Zwiebeln?	Do you really like _____ and onions?
Viele Matrosen standen auf der **Kaimauer**.	Lots of sailors stood on the _____ .
Das Spiel beginnt um 20 Uhr im **Stadion**.	The match starts at 8 pm in the _____ .
Jack schob den Rollstuhl **auf** die Fähre.	Jack pushed the wheelchair _____ the ferry.
Die 22 Spieler sind schon auf dem Fußbald**feld**.	The 22 players are already on the _____ .
Ich **interessiere mich für** Judo und Hockey.	_____ judo and hockey.
versuchen, einen Satz zu **umschreiben**	try to _____ a sentence

4 Word friends

In jedem Haus gibt es drei Wörter bzw. Wortverbindungen,
die man direkt nach dem Verb auf der Fahne benutzen kann.
Unterstreiche sie.

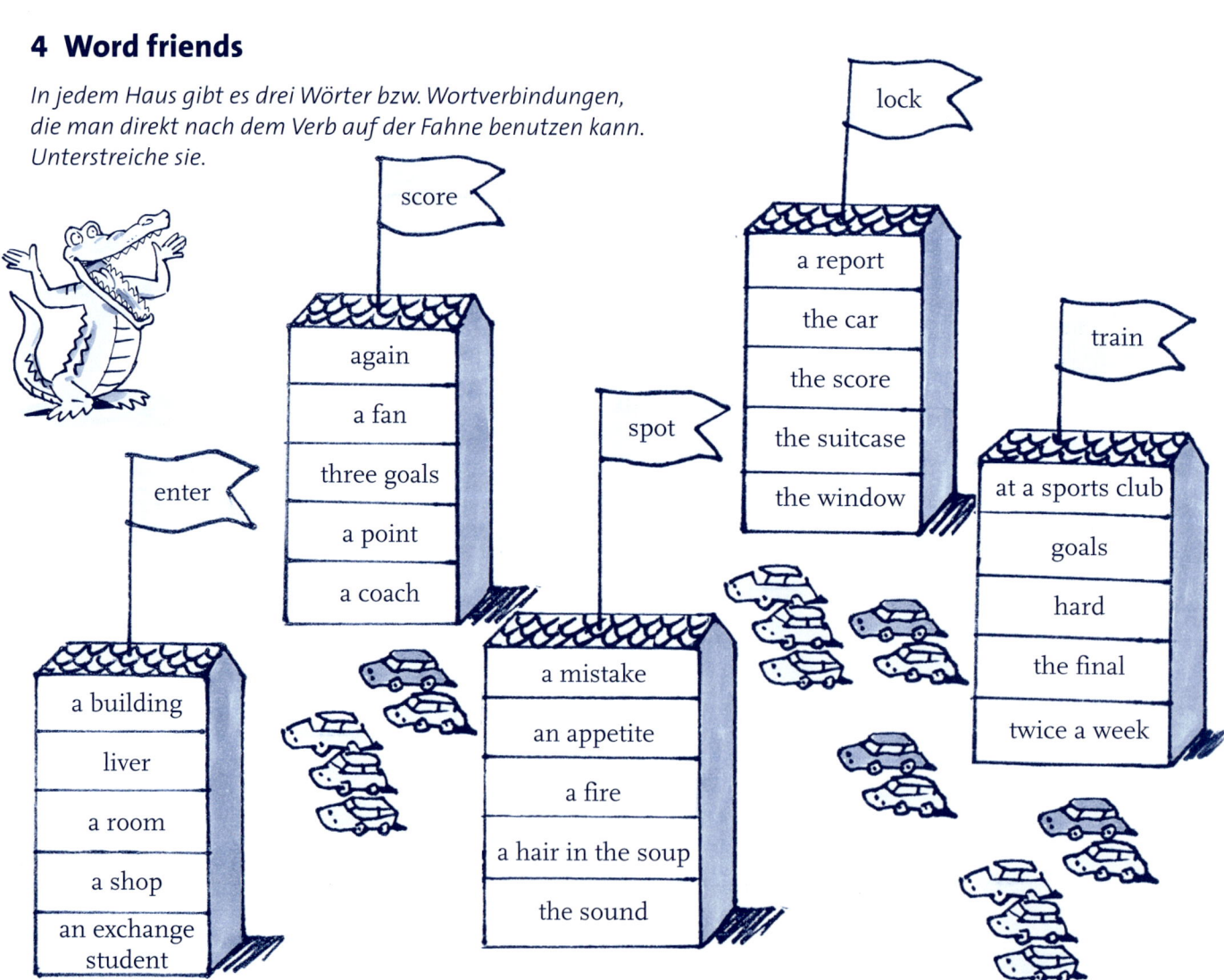

5 Classroom English

Welcher englische Satz ist korrekt – a, b oder c?

1 — Kann ich mit Klaus arbeiten?

a I work with Klaus? ☐

b Can I with Klaus work? ☐

c Can I work with Klaus? ☐

2 — Wer ist dran?

a Whose turn is it? ☐

b Where is on? ☐

c Who is on? ☐

3 — Du bist dran.

a You're on! ☐

b It's your turn. ☐

c It's you turn. ☐

6 Definitions

Vervollständige die Definitionen mit Wörtern aus den Mauersteinen. Trage die richtigen Wörter aus der Sprühwolke in die rechte Spalte ein.

clone   hostel
final   quay
head teacher   fan

eat   ship
looks   last   matches
most   person   hotel   school
team   place   winner

1 the __place__ at a harbour where you can get on (or off) a _____   __quay__

2 a person who _____ like a copy of another _____   _____

3 a person who really likes a _____ , wears team colours, goes to _____   _____

4 the _____ match – the _____ is the champion   _____

5 a kind of _____ where you can _____ and sleep cheaply   _____

6 the _____ important teacher at a _____   _____

New words ▸ *pp. 56–57*

Er ist nicht sehr **sportlich** – Er bewegt sich nie.	He isn't very _____ – he never moves.
Denkst du, er wird **fit** sein für das Spiel?	Do you think he'll be _____ for the match?
Wir spielen **gegen** die beste Mannschaft.	We're playing _____ the best team.
Warum hat Smith kein **Tor geschossen**?	Why didn't Smith _____ ?
Nach 45 Minuten war der **Spielstand** 2:1.	After 45 minutes the _____ was 2:1.
Die Fans jubelten, als Black ein **Tor** schoss.	The fans cheered when Black scored a _____ .
Wer hat den Schwimm**wettbewerb** gewonnen?	Who won the swimming _____ ?
In unserem Verein **trainieren** wir jeden Montag.	In our club we _____ every Monday.
Ist der **Trainer** böse auf seine Spieler?	Is the _____ angry with his players?
Können wir diese Mannschaft **schlagen**?	Can we _____ this team?
Am Ende waren wir die bessere Mannschaft.	_____ we were the better team.
Kannst du mir sagen, was dieses Wort **bedeutet**?	Can you tell me what this word _____ ?
einen **Pokal** gewinnen	win a _____
Der **Torwart** hat den Ball gehalten.	The _____ held the ball.

7 Word ladder

Gehe von unten nach oben, indem du bei jeder Sprosse einen Buchstaben veränderst.

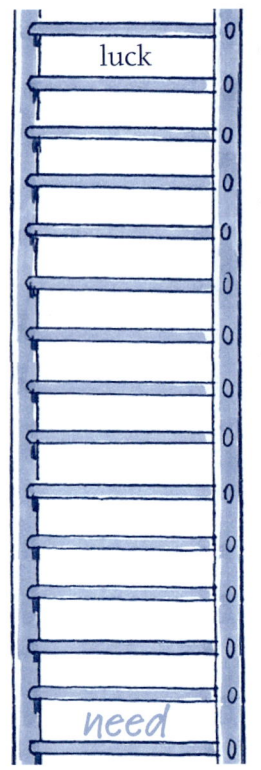

luck

need

Good ★ in your English test tomorrow.

Please close the windows and ★ them before you leave.

I can't find my key. Can you help me ★ for it?

prepare hot meals

I ★ some photos with my new camera yesterday.

How many pages are there in that ★ ?

The English word for Fußballschuh is football ★.

You can travel on water with this.

Manchester United ★ Bayern Munich 2:1.

★ from a cow is called beef.

Let's ★ tomorrow at 4 o'clock.

one foot – two ★

give food to an animal or person

The show is free, so we don't ★ any tickets.

8 What are the words?

*Finde für jeden Satz ein passendes deutsches Wort. Übersetze es und setze es ein. Wähle dann die richtige Form des Verbs **be**.*

> Nicht vergessen! Es gibt Wörter, die im Deutschen Plural sein können, im Englischen aber immer Einzahl sind.

Verkehrsmittel   Nachrichten   Hausaufgaben   Haare   Informationen

1 All the _information_ about Manchester __is__ in the brochure. (is/are)

2 Yesterday's Maths _____ _____ so hard – I wasn't able to do it all. (were/was)

3 What colour _____ Latisha's _____ ? Black or dark brown? (are/is)

4 _____ here _____ very good. The buses are always late. (isn't/aren't)

5 What time _____ the next _____ on TV? (is/are)

9 Pronunciation

Ordne die Wörter aus der Box der richtigen Aussprachegruppe zu.

> Englische Aussprache ist nicht immer einfach …

> Die Buchstaben OU, zum Beispiel, spricht man sehr unterschiedlich aus.

> Die Lautschriftsymbole im Dictionary helfen immer.

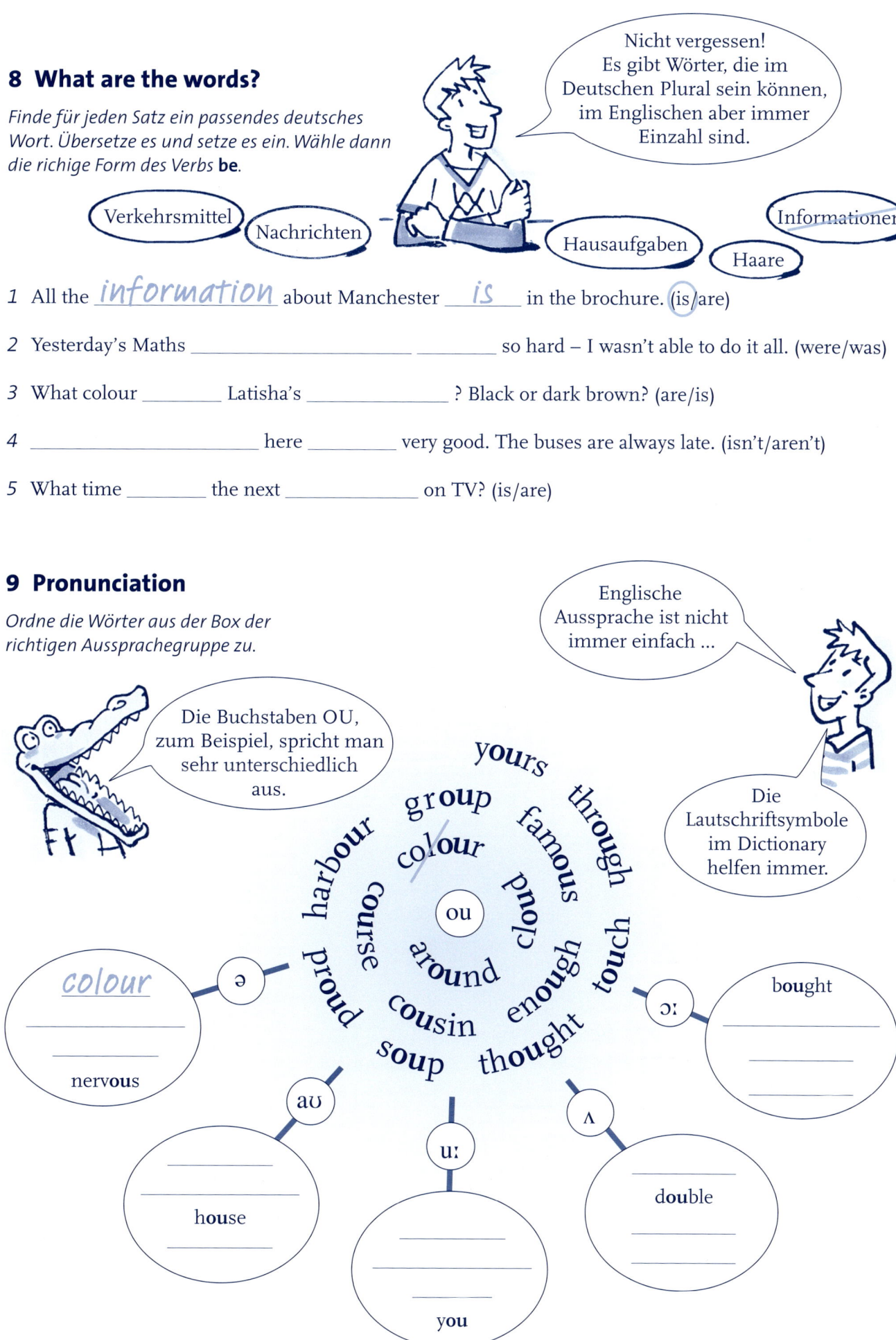

New words ▸ pp. 60–65

Die **Betonung** liegt auf der zweiten Silbe.   The _____ is on the second syllable.

Ich esse nie Leber oder **Niere**.   I never eat liver or _____ .

Kannst du das Essen und Trinken **organisieren**?   Can you _____ food and drinks?

interessante Ideen und **Gedanken**   interesting ideas and _____

Der Spielstand zur **Halbzeit** war 1:1.   The score at _____ was one all.

Wir essen drei **Mahlzeiten** am Tag.   We eat three _____ a day.

Kann ich bitte etwas **Kartoffelbrei** haben?   Can I have some _____ , please?

Bedien dich!   _____ !

11 Crossword

Wörter, die im Deutschen zusammengeschrieben werden, schreibt man im Englischen häufig auseinander. Wie viele dieser Wörter findest du im Rätsel? Die dicken Striche helfen dir.

Across →
1 Stadion (7)
3 Badeanzug (8)
4 Tor (5)
6 Meisterschaft (12)
8 Pokal (3)
11 Schläger (Tischtennis) (3)
12 Federball (9)
15 schlagen (4)
16 a Schläger (Tennis) (6)
18 Sattel (6)
19 Fan (3)
20 Endspiel (5)

Down ↓
1 Badehose (zwei Wörter: 8, 6)
2 Wettbewerb (11)
5 Spielstand (5)
7 trainieren (5)
9 Schützer, Schulterpolster (4)
10 erste Halbzeit (zwei Wörter: 5, 4)
13 Trainer (5)
14 Spiel (4)
17 Mannschaft (4)

11 More about ... Manchester United

Vervollständige den Text mit den Wörtern aus der Box.

~~club~~ even huge learn
match millions over rich
players third than times

Manchester United is a famous English football _club_. (1) They've been football champions of England 16 _____ (2) and, in 1968, they were the first English club to win the European Cup. In 2008 they won it a _____ (3) time. ManU isn't just popular in England. All _____ (4) the world, the club has _____ (5) of supporters. And it is very _____ (6), so it has enough money to buy the best _____ (7) (like Wayne Rooney or Cristiano Ronaldo). ManU's home is the _____ (8) stadium at Old Trafford, with room for 75,000 fans to watch a _____ . (9) The club has _____ (10) got a museum. More _____ (11) 200,000 visitors go there every year to _____ (12) about ManU's great past.

12 Last letter – first letter

Der letzte Buchstabe von jedem Wort ist gleichzeitig der erste des nächsten Wortes.

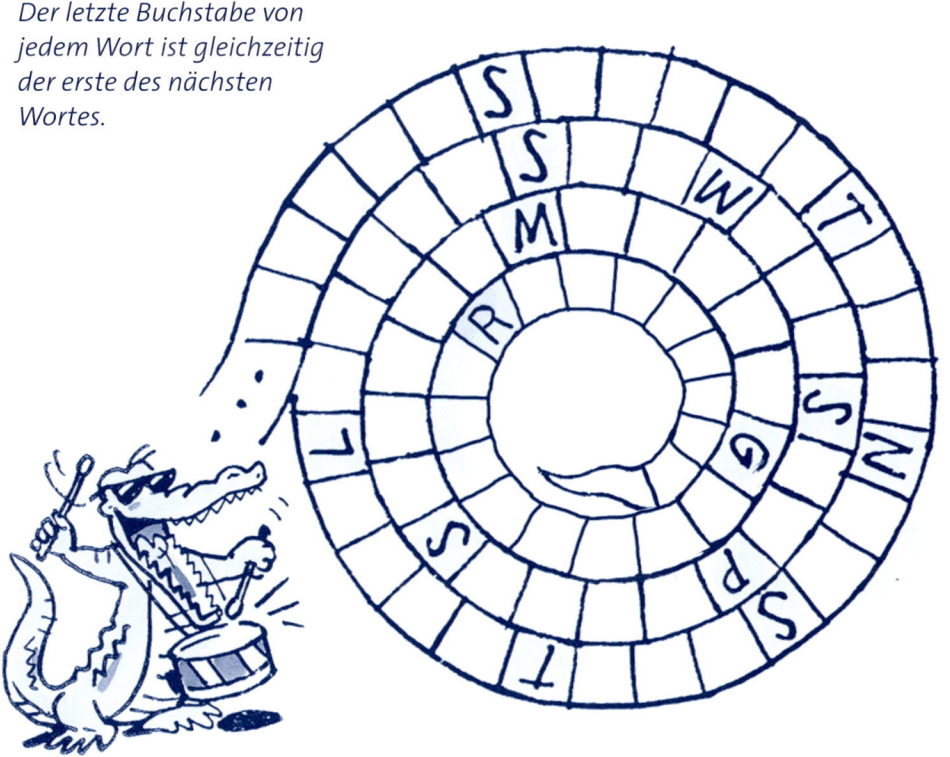

1 Betonung
2 Schulfach
3 trainieren
4 Nachrichten
5 Hemd
6 reisen
7 Unterricht
8 zeigen
9 Wörter
10 Schiff
11 Zeitungen
12 Stadion
13 Bedeutung
14 Torwart
15 wirklichkeitsnah

New words ▸ *p. 66; p. 101*

Papa ist in einer großen Familie **aufgewachsen**.	Dad _____ in a big family.
Wo seid ihr? Ich kann euch **nicht mehr** sehen.	Where are you? I can ___ see you _____ .
Guck! Sue hat ihren Pferdeschwanz **abgeschnitten**.	Look! Sue has _____ her ponytail.
Ein Unfall! Ruf einen **Krankenwagen**!	An accident! Call an _____ !
Er gewann eine **Medaille** in **Leichtathletik**.	He won a _____ in _____ .
Was sind deine **Hoffnungen** für die Zukunft?	What are you _____ for the future?
Die Spieler mussten hart **um** den Titel **kämpfen**.	The players had to _____ hard ___ the title.
Die **Operation** hat ihm das Leben gerettet.	The _____ saved his life.
Sind diese Blumen **künstlich** oder echt?	Are these flowers _____ or real?
Er ist schon immer **verrückt auf** Fußball gewesen.	He has always been _____ football.
Schnee! Nun kann ich meinen **Schlitten** benutzen.	Snow! Now I can use my _____ .
Ich benutze den Rollstuhl, weil ich **behindert** bin.	I use the wheelchair because I'm _____ .
Sie gewann eine Medaille bei den **Meisterschaften**.	She won a medal at the _____ .
Wie oft hat sie England **vertreten**?	How often did she _____ England?

13 Hour glasses

Übersetze die Wörter und trage sie in die passende Sanduhr ein.

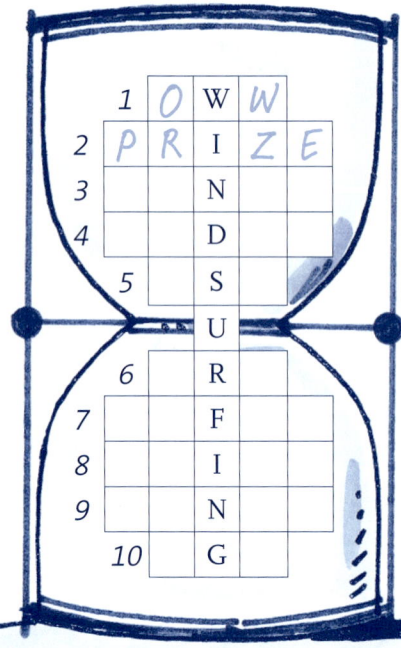

1 eigene(r,s) – ~~Ei~~
2 Spielstand – ~~Preis~~
3 Geld – trainieren
4 Lineal – Medaille
5 Ski laufen – fragen
6 versuchen – Geschlecht
7 Hoffnungen – fünfzig
8 jubeln – Punkt
9 Endspiel – groß
10 fragen – Alter

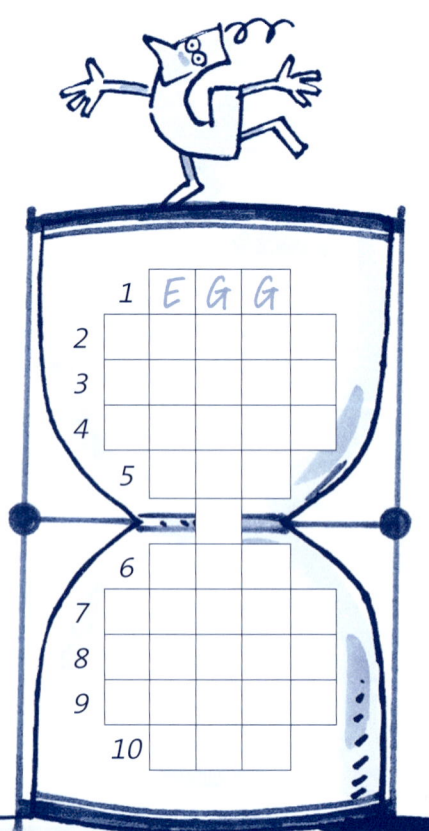

Linke Sanduhr:

1	O	W	W
2 P	R	I	Z E
3		N	
4		D	
5		S	
		U	
6		R	
7		F	
8		I	
9		N	
10		G	

Rechte Sanduhr:

1 E	G	G
2		
3		
4		
5		
6		
7		
8		
9		
10		

Das geheime Wort in der rechten Sanduhr heißt: Englisch _____

Deutsch _____

14 Word search

Finde Wörter im Rätsel, um die Wortgruppen zu vervollständigen. (↓ →)

I	B	M	A	C	H	Q	P	A	R	A	L	Y	M	P	I	C	S
X	G	E	G	H	S	A	L	A	D	X	G	O	A	L	Z	W	E
G	C	D	L	A	H	A	S	O	F	A	T	D	C	M	E	E	T
Q	J	A	T	I	O	C	U	P	R	T	R	Y	M	V	O	Z	D
A	Y	L	G	R	E	K	L	A	M	P	A	G	S	K	I	S	A
S	H	A	M	B	U	R	G	E	R	M	I	F	E	T	D	S	T
H	E	G	B	S	T	A	D	I	U	M	N	E	W	A	U	J	H
O	O	M	E	O	T	R	A	M	L	H	E	R	K	X	O	S	L
R	M	T	D	P	U	L	L	O	V	E	R	R	Y	I	S	P	E
T	R	O	U	S	E	R	S	A	I	U	S	Y	T	N	C	A	T
S	C	U	P	B	O	A	R	D	W	Q	R	P	O	R	K	G	I
H	S	S	L	J	A	C	P	S	A	U	S	A	G	E	T	H	C
D	H	O	I	N	N	H	L	Y	K	P	I	Z	Z	A	A	E	S
S	I	C	V	S	O	I	A	G	P	S	H	E	L	F	B	T	G
K	P	K	A	O	R	P	N	S	L	O	R	R	Y	V	L	T	N
I	W	N	B	U	A	S	E	W	A	R	D	R	O	B	E	I	Q
R	I	T	U	P	K	A	U	N	D	E	R	G	R	O	U	N	D
T	P	H	S	T	V	O	L	L	E	Y	B	A	L	L	Q	N	P

transport

_____
_____
_____
_____
_____
_____

sport

athletics

_____
_____
_____
_____
_____
_____

room

_____
_____
_____
_____
_____

clothes

_____
_____
_____
_____
_____

food

_____
_____
_____
_____
_____
_____

Unit 4

New words ▸ p. 69

Ich mag keine Hotels, daher **gingen** wir **zelten**.	I don't like hotels, so we _____ .
Wir **zelteten** auf einem Feld.	We _____ in a field.
Lass uns auf diesem Fluss **Kanu fahren gehen**.	Let's _____ on this river.
Auf diesem Fluss habe ich gelernt, **Kanu** zu **fahren**.	I learned to _____ on this river.
Wir sind nicht alt genug um **jagen** zu **gehen**.	We aren't old enough to _____ .
Ich kann nicht verstehen, warum sie Bären **jagen**.	I can't understand why they _____ bears.
im Winter **Schneeschuhwandern** gehen	_____ in deep snow
Schlafpartys in einem alten Haus **veranstalten**	_____ in an old house
Ich wollte nicht viel machen, nur **rumhängen**.	I didn't want to do much, just _____ .
Wir wohnten in einer **Hütte** in den Bergen.	We stayed in a _____ in the mountains.
Der Bär ist tot. Warum haben sie ihn **erschossen**?	The bear is dead. Why did they _____ it?

1 Classroom English

Welcher englische Satz ist korrekt – a, b oder c?

1. Wie heißt „sleepover" auf Deutsch?

   a What's 'sleepover' in German? ☐
   b What's 'sleepover' on German? ☐
   c How say you 'sleepover' in German? ☐

2. Auf welcher Seite sind wir, bitte?

   a What side we are on, please? ☐
   b What side are we on, please? ☐
   c What page are we on, please? ☐

3. Wie spricht man das erste Wort in Zeile 2 aus?

   a How say you the first word in line 2? ☐
   b How do you say the first word in line 2? ☐
   c How do you say the first word in lane 2? ☐

4. Können Sie es bitte an die Tafel schreiben?

   a Can you write it on the table, please? ☐
   b You can write it off the board, please? ☐
   c Can you write it on the board, please? ☐

2 School words

Ergänze die fehlenden Wörter. Finde das „geheime Wort" und übersetze es.

1 **b o a r d**   Jack, can you write the answers on the ★ please?

2 _ _ _ _ _   We have lots of good singers in our school ★.

3 _ _ _ _ _ _   I'm in the seventh ★ this year.

4 _ _ _ _ _ _ _ _   How many ★ are there at your school? – About 800.

5 _ _ _ _ _ _ _   In ★ you learn about the past.

6 _ _ _ _ _ _ _   And in ★ you learn about flowers, animals, etc.

7 _ _ _ _ _   I need a ★, not a pen.

8 _ _ _ _ _ _ _   We have the same ★ for PE and English: Mr Hill.

9 _ _ _   In ★ you learn how to draw and paint.

10 _ _ _ _ _   In English we have to write an ★ about our hobbies.

The secret word is: Englisch _____ Deutsch _____

3 Word pairs

Welche Wörter passen zusammen?

read

correct   score

climb

listen to

win   build

medal   call   turn on   wear   cook   grow

medal
ambulance
stadium
light
football shirt
a meal
lettuce
live music
magazine
mistake
mountain
goal

New words ▸ *pp. 70 – 71*

Ich hoffe, **Mama** und Papa werden kommen.	I hope _____ and dad will come.
Warum **darf** sie nicht zur Party gehen?	Why isn't she _____ go to the party?
Könntest du diese **Rechnung** für mich bezahlen?	Could you pay this _____ for me?
Es ist nicht meine Schuld, dass du kein Buch hast.	_____ that you don't have a book.
Unsere Eltern sind **streng**, aber fair.	Our parents are _____ , but fair.
Ich kann nicht kommen. Ich **habe Hausarrest**.	I can't come. I' _____ .
Vielleicht hast du beim Test gut **abgeschnitten**.	Maybe you _____ the test.
Dieser **altmodischer** Hut gehörte Opa.	This _____ hat was grandpa's.
Ich mag **moderne** Städte lieber als alte Städte.	I like _____ cities more than old cities.
Rote Jeans verstoßen gegen die **Kleiderordung**.	Red jeans are against the _____ .
Warum sind die **Regeln** so streng?	Why are the _____ so strict?
Ich habe nicht viel **Schmuck** – nur einen Ring.	I haven't much _____ – just a ring.
Kann ich ein **weites** Hemd anziehen,	Can I put on a _____ shirt
... wenn ich diese **enge** Jeans trage?	... if I wear these _____ jeans?
Gib mir nicht **die Schuld für** deine Fehler!	Don't _____ me _____ your mistakes.
modische **Unterwäsche** tragen	wear trendy _____
Dein Oberteil ist sehr kurz! Ich sehe deinen **Bauch**.	Your top's very short! I see your _____ .
Ich habe Hunger – mein Magen ist leer.	I'm hungry – my _____ is empty.

4 One or two letters?

*Trage die fehlenden Buchstaben ein: **g** oder **gg**, **l** oder **ll**, usw.*

g/gg	re_gg_ae, be____inning, lan____uage, ba____y, fo____, fo____y
l/ll	co____ect, adu____t, unti____, meda____, mode____, pu____over
m/mm	co____unity, swi____er, wo____an, gra____ar, mo____ent, thermo____eter
p/pp	re____ort, sho____ing, unha____y, a____etite, re____resent, disa____ear
r/rr	dia____y, ma____ied, guita____, ti____ed, hu____y, diffe____ent
s/ss	promi____e, e____ay, gla____es, gue____, hu____band, i____land
t/tt	bo____le, wa____er, pre____y, wea____her, spaghe____i

5 Vocabulary network

*Vervollständige das Wörternetz.
Die Verben, die auf den Zetteln
fehlen, bringt der Geier.
Die anderen Wörter findest du
im Sand.*

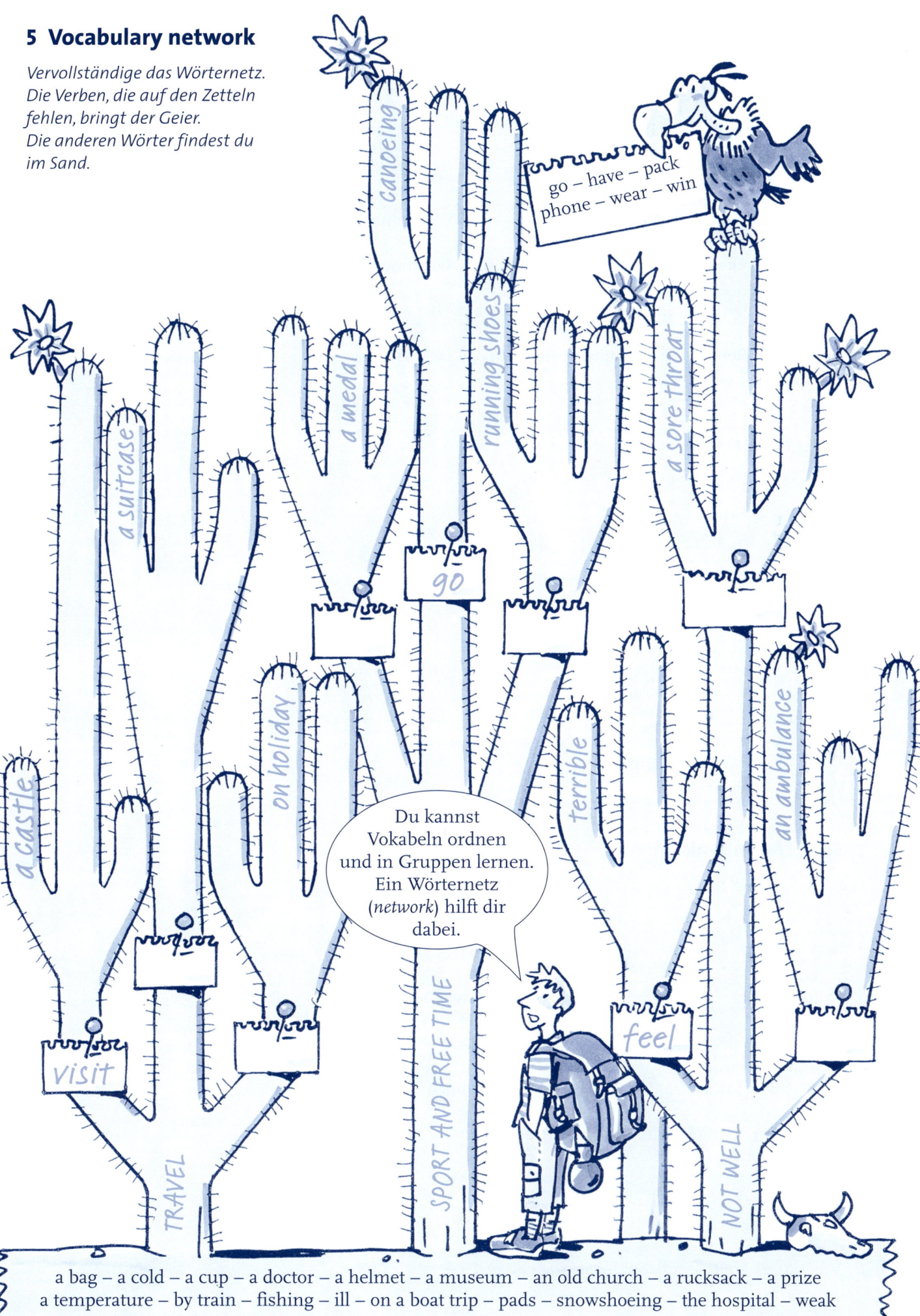

go – have – pack
phone – wear – win

canoeing

a medal

running shoes

a sore throat

a suitcase

go

a castle

on holiday

terrible

an ambulance

Du kannst
Vokabeln ordnen
und in Gruppen lernen.
Ein Wörternetz
(*network*) hilft dir
dabei.

visit

SPORT AND FREE TIME

feel

TRAVEL

NOT WELL

a bag – a cold – a cup – a doctor – a helmet – a museum – an old church – a rucksack – a prize
a temperature – by train – fishing – ill – on a boat trip – pads – snowshoeing – the hospital – weak

New words ▸ *pp. 72 – 73*

Hey **Leute**! Wartet auf mich!	Hey _____ ! Wait for me!
Ich denke, er wird **bis** 8 Uhr hier sein.	I think he'll be here _____ 8 o'clock.
Bitte **brainstormt** so viele Ideen wie möglich.	Please _____ as many ideas as possible.
Wer ist der **Leiter** dieser Gruppe?	Who's the _____ of this group?
Wir kennen **uns** – wir sind alte Freunde.	We know _____ – we're old friends.
Die **Bühne** ist zu klein für so viele Schauspieler.	The _____ is too small for so many actors.
Lass uns den **Refrain** zusammensingen.	Let's sing the _____ together.

6 Verb forms

Ergänze die Tabelle der unregelmäßigen Verben.

1	do	did	done		7			found
2			beaten		8	grow	grew	
3	break				9			forgotten
4		cut			10	let		
5	draw				11		meant	
6		fought			12	upset		

7 Spot the mistakes

In jedem Satz sind zwei Fehler. Unterstreiche und korrigiere sie.

1 When <u>childs</u> are young they often have teddy beers. *children* _____

2 Bears can look realy sweet and lots off people love them. _____ _____

3 But they are allso large and very danger animals. _____ _____

4 They usualy hunt at night or in the errly morning. _____ _____

5 Bears can ran quickly and they are great swimers. _____ _____

6 It's very interresting to watch how a bear catchs fish. _____ _____

7 It stand in the river and waits quitely for a long time. _____ _____

8 When the bare sees a fish it jump and catches it. _____ _____

4 · 41

8 Word search

Im Rätsel sind 28 Tiere versteckt.
Finde und schreibe sie auf. (↓ →)

hedgehog

L	S	J	E	C	G	H	E	D	G	E	H	O	G	C
I	Q	F	L	H	I	O	V	X	R	S	N	A	K	E
O	U	O	E	I	R	M	H	M	H	T	M	N	X	S
N	I	X	P	C	A	O	O	A	I	S	B	H	R	C
S	R	F	H	K	F	U	R	I	N	E	S	C	O	F
H	R	X	A	E	F	S	S	M	O	N	K	E	Y	Y
E	E	Z	N	N	E	E	C	Y	W	A	E	S	U	
E	L	K	T	P	I	G	K	K	Z	I	N	H	F	G
P	F	F	S	B	O	B	C	Y	A	B	G	A	I	B
Q	R	T	N	Y	S	E	S	L	D	P	A	M	S	U
Y	O	U	G	F	X	A	M	O	L	E	R	S	H	D
P	G	R	C	O	W	R	P	A	R	R	O	T	N	G
V	Z	K	G	O	F	P	H	I	P	P	O	E	K	I
K	X	E	C	R	O	C	O	D	I	L	E	R	W	E
X	H	Y	G	R	A	B	B	I	T	I	G	E	R	Y

9 Pronunciation

In jeder Wortgruppe gibt es ein Wort mit einem stummen Buchstaben. Finde das Wort und streiche den stummen Buchstaben durch.

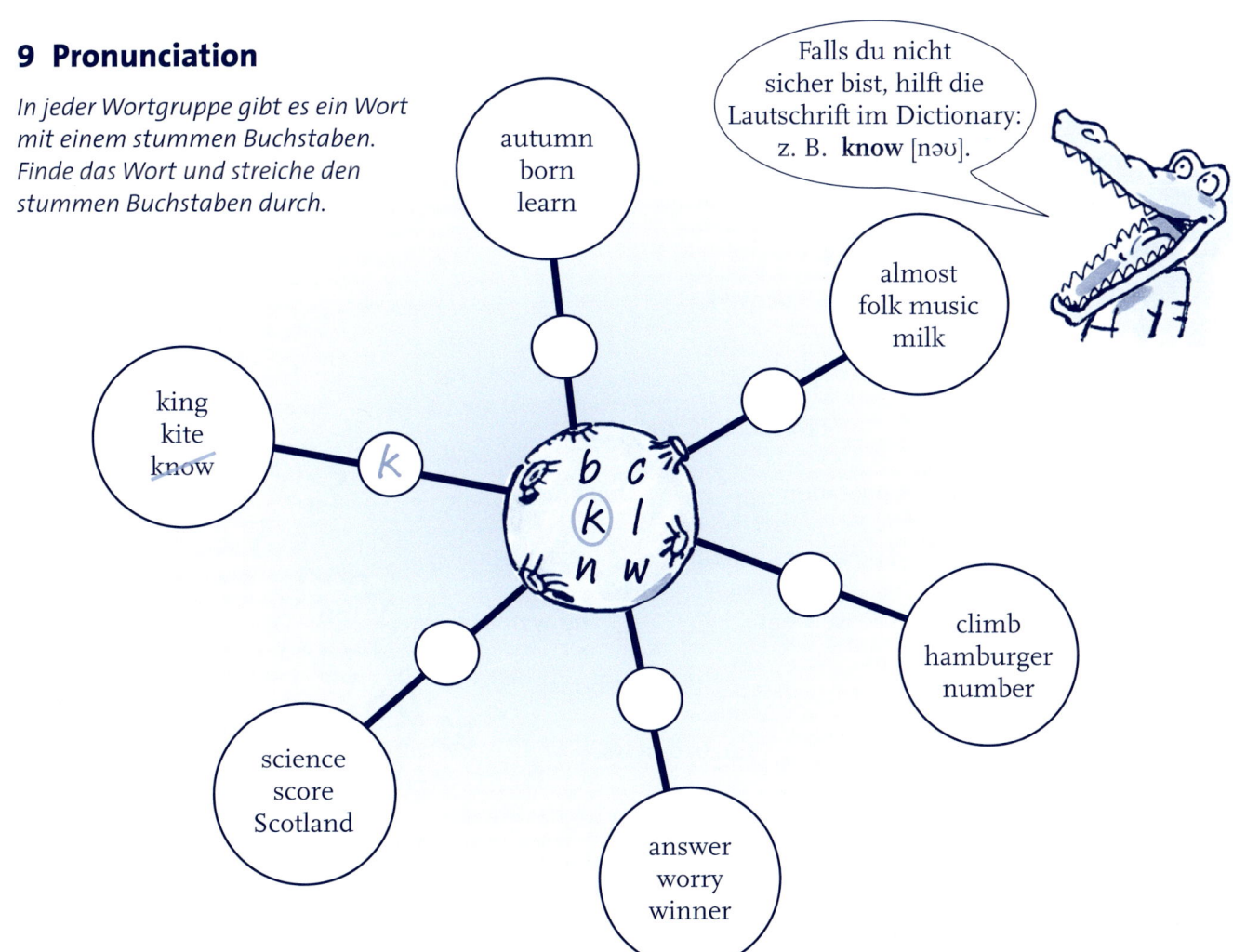

Falls du nicht sicher bist, hilft die Lautschrift im Dictionary: z. B. **know** [nəʊ].

autumn
born
learn

almost
folk music
milk

king
kite
know

b c
k l
n w

climb
hamburger
number

science
score
Scotland

answer
worry
winner

New words ▸ *pp. 76 – 80*

Über 10 **Prozent** der Briten leben in London.	Over 10 _____ of the British live in London.
Die Zimmer kosten 50 Euro **pro** Nacht.	The rooms cost 50 euros _____ night.
Der See ist 14 **Kilometer** lang.	The lake ist 14 _____ long.
Wieviele **Zentimeter** hat ein Meter?	How many _____ are there in a metre?
ein 30 **Kilogramm** schwerer Hund	a 30-_____ dog
Sie sieht nicht aus wie eine **Vierzehnjährige**.	She doesn't look like a _____ .
einen **vierzehnjährigen** Jungen kennen	know a _____ boy
Mehr als zwei **Millionen** Menschen leben hier.	More than two _____ people live here.
Es ist gesünder, keinen Tabak zu **rauchen**.	It's healthier not to _____ tobacco.
Wo **Rauch** ist, ist auch Feuer.	Where there's _____ , there's fire.
für mehr Geld **streiken**	go on _____ for more money
Das Wetter wird **nass** und windig werden.	The weather will be _____ and windy.
Wolltest du nicht deinen Aufsatz **überarbeiten**?	Didn't you want to _____ your essay?
die **Rechtschreibung** in einem Aufsatz überprüfen	check the _____ in an essay
Wir hörten einen **Dialog** zwischen zwei Mädchen.	We heard a _____ between two girls.

10 Lost words

Ergänze die Sätze mit den Wörtern im Feuerwerk.

1 She looked __*at*__ me and smiled.

2 ManU is playing _____ Liverpool FC today.

3 Jack is in hospital for an operation _____ his knee.

4 If you wait _____ Sue arrives, you'll be able to say hello.

5 It was cold in the garden so we went _____ and watched TV.

6 We live in the city centre _____ the big shops.

7 Mike was very upset _____ the bad news.

8 Anna moved her English books _____ a higher shelf.

9 We have to get _____ the train at the next station.

10 I didn't like the party at first, but _____ the end it was OK.

(firework words: until, on, against, at, about, off, in, onto, near, inside)

11 Odd word out

Finde und unterstreiche das Wort, das nicht passt.

1 kilometre – minute – metre – centimetre

2 chorus – drawing – photo – picture

3 seven – per cent – eight – nine

4 leg – foot – shoe – knee

5 eyes – build – glasses – see

6 adults – children – teenagers – sledges

7 shop – gig – supermarket – department store

8 journey – ride – trip – coast

12 The fourth word

Welches Wort fehlt hier?

1 one – thousand / metre – _____

2 sing – singer / play – _____

3 he – they / himself – _____

4 green – colour / two – _____

5 parrot – bird / piano – _____

6 days – month / months – _____

7 day – sun / night – _____

8 man – men / woman – _____

13 More about ... traditional Inuit hunting

Vervollständige den Text mit Wörtern aus der Box.

The Inuit live in Greenland and in the north of Canada, where winter *temperatures* (1) can be minus 40 degrees Celsius. So it's _____ (2) too cold to have farm animals or to grow food. That's why hunting and _____ (3) were once a very big part of Inuit life. The meat of sea animals like the walrus or the whale, or of _____ (4) animals like the polar bear, was traditional Inuit food. And of course, hunting wasn't _____ (5) important for food. The Inuit could also use animal *skins to make clothes. In the past, when the Inuit hunted sea animals they used a *kayak*, a _____ (6) of canoe. And on land they _____ (7) sledges with dogs. A team of dogs could easily pull 20 kilos. And dogs _____ (8) smell very well too, so they could help the Inuit to find the animals. Sometimes a hunting trip took a few days, so the Inuit often _____ (9) little igloos when they needed a place to sleep at night. Inside an igloo, the temperature could be quite warm when it was very _____ (10) outside.

built	cold	could	fishing
just	kind	land	much
	temperatures	used	

minus = minus; walrus = Walross; whale = Wal; polar bear = Eisbär; traditional = traditionell; skin = Fell, Haut; igloo = Iglu

New words ▸ *pp. 81–82*

einen interessanten Zeitungs**artikel** lesen	read an interesting newspaper _____
mit **Messer** und **Gabel** essen	eat with a _____ and _____
Haben viele Menschen den **Angriff** überlebt?	Did many people survive the _____ ?
Warum **greifen** Bären Menschen an?	Why do bears _____ people?
Hat jemand angerufen, **während** ich weg war?	Did anybody phone _____ I was out?
den **Opfern** eines Unfalls helfen.	help the _____ of an accident
Kennst du ihr **neuestes** Lied?	Do you know their _____ song?
Es gab ein Feuer, aber wir konnten **entkommen**.	There was a fire, but we were able to _____ .

14 Crossword

Across ➡
1 You use this to cut things. (5)
4 It isn't healthy to ★ tobacco. (5)
6 German – Dialog / English – ★ (8)
7 The bear ran after us, but we were able to ★. (6)
9 We have to sing the ★ four times in this song. (6)
12 under 18 – child / 18 or older – ★ (5)
13 German – Gruppenleiter / English – group ★ (6)
15 a small house in a forest or in the mountains (5)
16 when people stop work because they want more money. (6)

Down ⬇
1 description – describe / revision – ★ (6)
2 German – beliebt / English – ★ (7)
4 You need snowshoes to do this sport. (11)
5 another word for 'newest' (6)
8 German – sich streiten / English – ★ (5)
10 Jake isn't allowed to stay up late at weekends – he's got very ★ parents. (6)
11 If you ★ people, you try to hurt or kill them. (6)
14 After it rains, the ground is ★. (3)

15 Word groups

Trage die Wörter aus der Wolke in die richtigen Sterne ein.

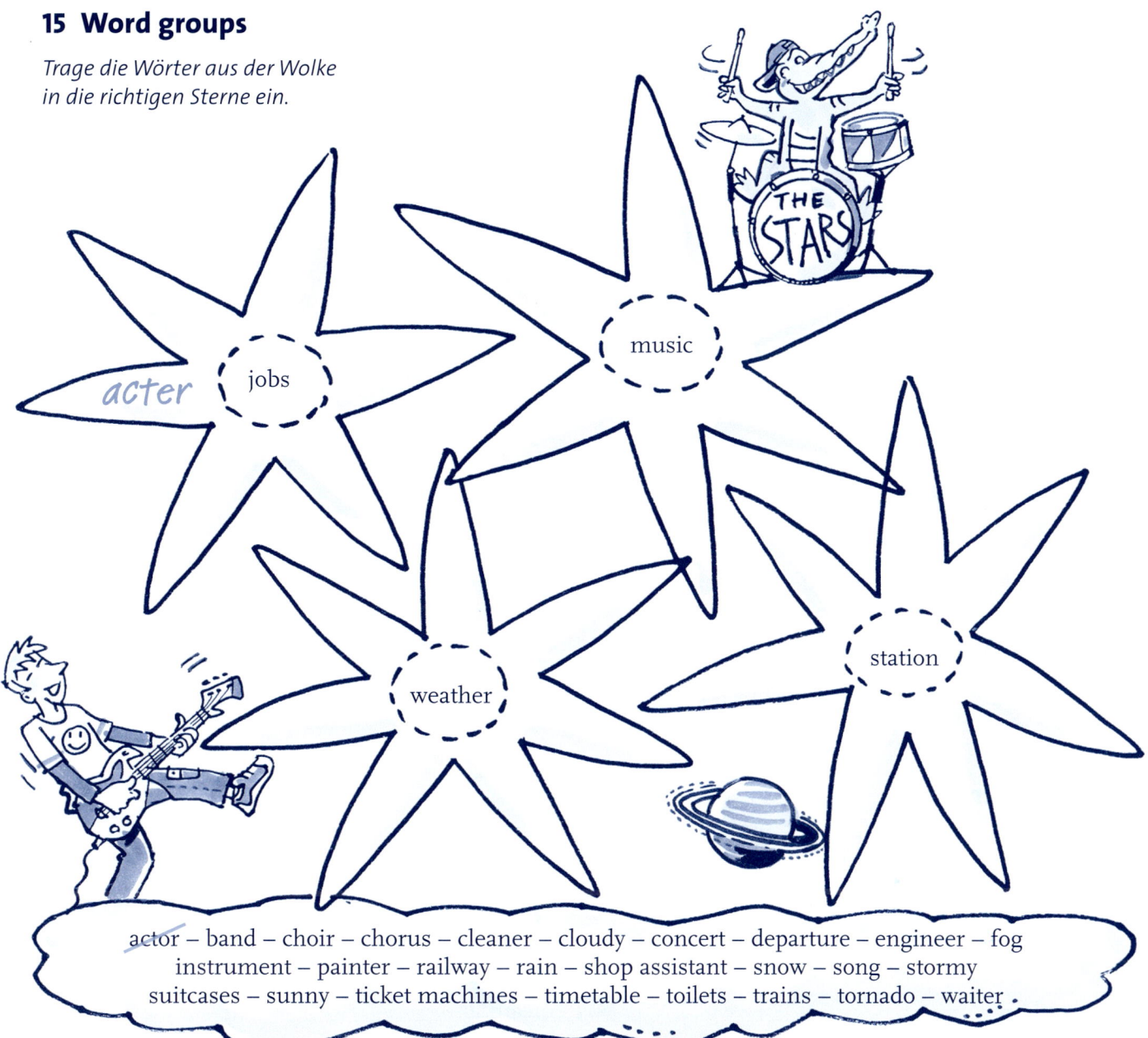

jobs

acter

music

weather

station

actor – band – choir – chorus – cleaner – cloudy – concert – departure – engineer – fog
instrument – painter – railway – rain – shop assistant – snow – song – stormy
suitcases – sunny – ticket machines – timetable – toilets – trains – tornado – waiter

16 Opposites

Trage die Gegenteile der fettgedruckten Wörter in die Lücken ein.

1 have a **tidy** / _____ room

2 expensive / _____ clothes

3 wear **old-fashioned** / _____ clothes

4 turn the radio **on** / _____

5 **over** / _____ 20 per cent

6 **enter** / _____ the classroom

7 at the **top** / _____ of the shelf

8 **forget** / _____ an important date

9 There are 90 **arrivals** / _____ every day.

10 find a **husband** / _____

11 an **exciting** / a _____ film

12 a really **hot** / _____ day

13 a **clean** / _____ city

14 Wait **downstairs** / _____ in your room!

Unit 5

New words ▸ *pp. 88–89*

Was **produziert** diese Fabrik?	What does this factory _____ ?
Ein **Redakteur** überprüft und korrigiert Texte.	An _____ checks and corrects texts.
ein **Künstler**, der Städe malt	an _____ who paints cities
Fotografen haben oft große Kameras.	_____ often have big cameras.
Wer wir der Bericht **veröffentlichen**?	Who's going to _____ the report?
Das musst du selbst entscheiden.	_____
Wir können ein Foto oder eine **Zeichnung** benutzen.	We can use a photo or a _____ .
Als erstes musst du eine Linie **zeichnen**.	First you have to _____ a line.
einen guten **Film** im Kino anschauen	watch a good _____ in the cinema
Jazz ist OK, aber **am meisten mag ich** Rock.	Jazz is OK, but _____ rock _____ .

1 Word families

Finde die passenden Verben zu den angegebenen Nomen.

1 drawing – *draw*_____

2 revision – _____

3 spelling – _____

4 drawing – _____

5 explanation – _____

6 life – _____

7 attack – _____

8 meaning – _____

9 recording – _____

10 laughter – _____

2 The best word

Finde das Wort in der Strickleiter, das am besten in die Lücke passt.

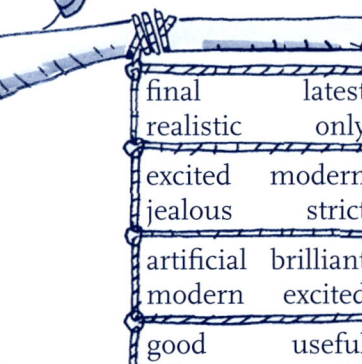

final	latest
realistic	only

excited	modern
jealous	strict

artificial	brilliant
modern	excited

good	useful
silly	successful

1 Today's the _____ day of the holidays. Tomorrow we go back to school.

2 My friend's parents are really _____ . He always has to go to bed early.

3 Are those flowers real or _____ ?

4 What a _____ idea! It will never work!

3 Last letter – first letter

Der letzte Buchstabe von jedem Wort ist gleichzeitig der erste des nächsten Wortes.

1 Refrain
2 Bauch
3 Jagd
4 Zwillinge
5 streng
6 Hose
7 Schreibung, Schreibweise
8 Oma
9 Publikum
10 Redakteur
11 überarbeiten, wiederholen
12 elektrisch
13 Currygericht
14 ja
15 Abschnitt

4 The fourth word

Welches Wort wird hier gesucht?

1 banana – fruit / pea – _____

2 lunch – meal / chicken curry – _____

3 London – city / UK – _____

4 Friday – day / August – _____

5 castle – building / piano – _____

6 Britain – island / Uranus – _____

7 seven – number / pink – _____

8 song – music/ drawing – _____

5 Pronunciation

Ordne die Wörter aus der Box der richtigen Aussprachegruppe zu.

ʊ   juː   ʌ

bully but computer community excuse full fun huge menu
publish pull push put sugar summer trumpet tub tunnel

bully_____   computer_____   fun_____

_____   _____   _____

_____   _____   _____

_____   _____   _____

_____   _____   _____

New words ▸ p. 90

Überfliegt den Text, aber lest ihn nicht im Detail.   _____ the text, but don't read it in detail.

Diese Zeitung hat einen tollen Sport**teil**.   This paper has a great sport _____ .

Jeder mag ihn – er ist sehr **beliebt**.   Everybody likes him – he's very _____ .

6 Word building

Verbinde ein Wort aus der Liste mit
einem Wort auf den Noten.
Trage die deutsche Übersetzung ein.

> Eine Regel gibt's
> leider nicht.
> Also merkt euch die
> Einzelfälle!

> Wenn man
> Nomen miteinander
> verbindet, schreibt man
> sie mal auseinander,
> mal zusammen.

instant · chat · text · running · north · class · car · snow · semi · bed

1 _running_ shoes   _Laufschuhe_   6 _semi-_ final   _____

2 _____ park   _____   7 _____ east   _____

3 _chat_ room   _____   8 _bed_ room   _____

4 _____ message   _____   9 _____ shoes   _____

5 _____ message   _____   10 _____ mate   _____

7 Making phrases

Vervollständige die Audrücke mit einem Verb
von den Zetteln.

1 _turn_   on the radio

2 _____ my bedroom once a week

3 _____ vocabulary for the next test

4 _____ to my classmates about the weekend

5 _____ up in a big city

6 _____ up a word I don't know

7 _____ from a fire in a hotel

8 _____ with my partner's ideas

grow · agree · escape · revise · turn · tidy · look · talk

8 Hour glasses

Übersetze die Wörter und trage sie in die passende Sanduhr ein.

1 S P Y
2 S M O K E
3   O L I
4
5   C
     E
6   W
7   O
8   M
9   A
10   N

1 A C T
2
3
4
5
6
7
8
9
10

1 Spion / aufführen, spielen
2 Schaf – rauchen
3 Kanu – Schultyrann
4 während – Meter
5 Eis – Auftritt
6 eigene(r,s) – Geschlecht
7 beobachten – schießen
8 Lämmer – Lastwagen
9 raten – Bühne
10 Schluss – fragen

Das geheime Wort in der rechten Sanduhr heißt: Englisch _____

Deutsch _____

9 Word search - The media

*15 englische Begriffe aus dem Wortfeld „Medien"
sind im Rätsel versteckt.
Finde sie und übersetze sie ins Deutsche. (↓ →)*

monitor – Bildschirm

_____

_____

_____

_____

_____

_____

_____

_____

_____

_____

_____

_____

_____

E	Z	M	O	N	I	T	O	R	H	P	C
D	M	A	G	A	Z	I	N	E	E	U	Q
I	K	Z	W	B	H	X	N	A	B	T
T	O	J	E	O	P	R	A	E	M	L	M
O	R	E	C	O	R	D	R	W	A	I	O
R	H	V	D	K	O	R	T	S	I	S	B
Y	E	L	Z	S	G	E	I	P	L	H	I
G	F	R	T	U	R	P	C	A	N	X	L
R	A	D	I	O	A	O	L	P	E	B	E
N	Z	D	G	K	M	R	E	E	S	G	H
W	N	E	W	S	M	T	Q	R	D	V	W
S	U	T	E	L	E	V	I	S	I	O	N

New words ▶ p. 91

Wie lang sind die Sommer**ferien** in Kanada?	How long is summer _____ in Canada?
Bist du auch **gut in** Französisch?	Are you _____ French too?
eine **Rolle** in einem Film spielen	play a _____ in a movie
eine **Karriere** als Ingenieur	a _____ as an engineer
Er ist **Kapitän** der Schul-Hockeymannschaft.	He's _____ of the school hockey team.
Interesse an einem neuen Buch zeigen	show _____ in a new book

10 Classroom English

Welcher englische Satz ist korrekt – a, b oder c?

1 Kannst du bitte lauter sprechen?

a Can you tell louder, please? ☐
b Can you louder speak, please? ☐
c Can you speak louder, please? ☐

2 Kannst du Übung Nummer 3 lösen?

a Can you exercise number 3? ☐
b Can you lose exercise number three? ☐
c Can you find exercise number three? ☐

3 Ich bin mir nicht sicher.

a I'm not sure. ☐
b I'm myself not safe. ☐
c I'm myself not sure. ☐

4 Ich stimme Tanja zu.

a I agree not with Tanja. ☐
b I agree with Tanja. ☐
c I agree to Tanja. ☐

15 Hidden words

Ergänze die Wortgruppen, indem du Wörter mit Buchstaben der Wörter „musical instruments" bildest.

musical instruments = Musikinstrumente

16 Word ladder

Gehe von unten nach oben, indem du bei jeder Sprosse einen Buchstaben veränderst.

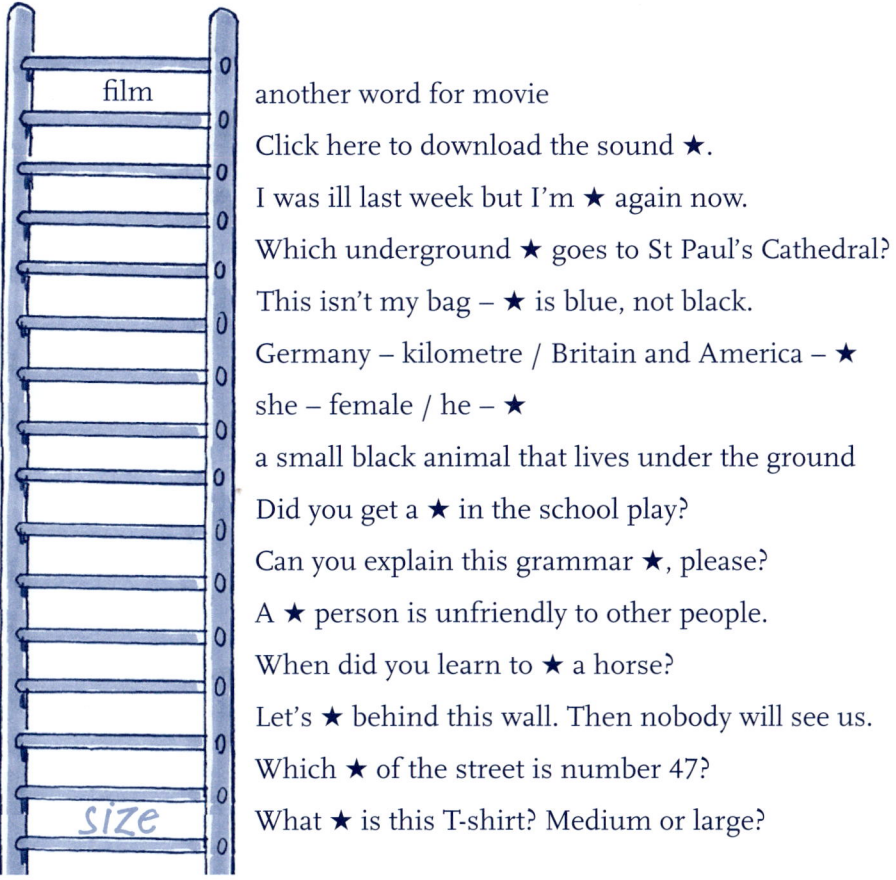

another word for movie

Click here to download the sound ★.

I was ill last week but I'm ★ again now.

Which underground ★ goes to St Paul's Cathedral?

This isn't my bag – ★ is blue, not black.

Germany – kilometre / Britain and America – ★

she – female / he – ★

a small black animal that lives under the ground

Did you get a ★ in the school play?

Can you explain this grammar ★, please?

A ★ person is unfriendly to other people.

When did you learn to ★ a horse?

Let's ★ behind this wall. Then nobody will see us.

Which ★ of the street is number 47?

What ★ is this T-shirt? Medium or large?

17 Word friends

Welche Wörter auf den Steinen passen in die Lücken?

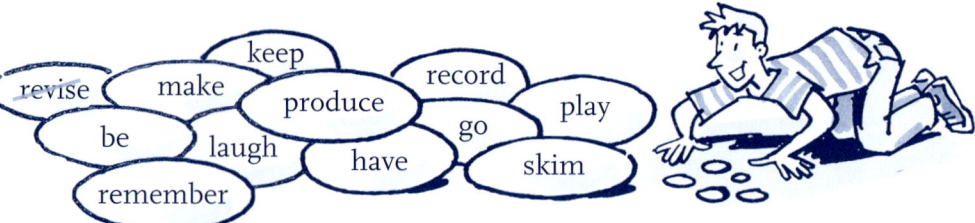

keep · revise · make · produce · record · play · be · laugh · go · have · skim · remember

1 _revise_ a text / grammar / vocabulary

2 _____ a newspaper / cars / computers

3 _____ a point / a phone call / a mess

4 _____ a new CD / a single / a song

5 _____ the drums / hockey / outside

6 _____ on strike / to school / shopping

7 _____ good at sth. / strict / in time

8 _____ a cold / a party / fun

9 _____ at a joke / quietly / loudly

10 _____ an article / the first page / the report

11 _____ in touch / sth. warm / fit

12 _____ a great day / somebody / to call me

18 Odd word out

Finde und unterstreiche das Wort, das nicht passt.

1 artist – painter – picture – photographer

2 book – magazine – newspaper – publish

3 pen – rubber – section – pencil sharpener

4 draw – whistle – speak – sing

5 read – score – scan – skim

6 curry – crisps – carrot – career

7 plane – captain – car – train

8 awful – horrible – popular – terrible

9 drawing – felt tip – pen – pencil

10 mail – movie – instant message – text message

19 Scrambled words: American and British English

Die Buchstabenrätsel ergeben Wörter aus dem amerikanischen Englisch. Trage diese und ihre britischen Entsprechungen ein. Die Tipps helfen dir.

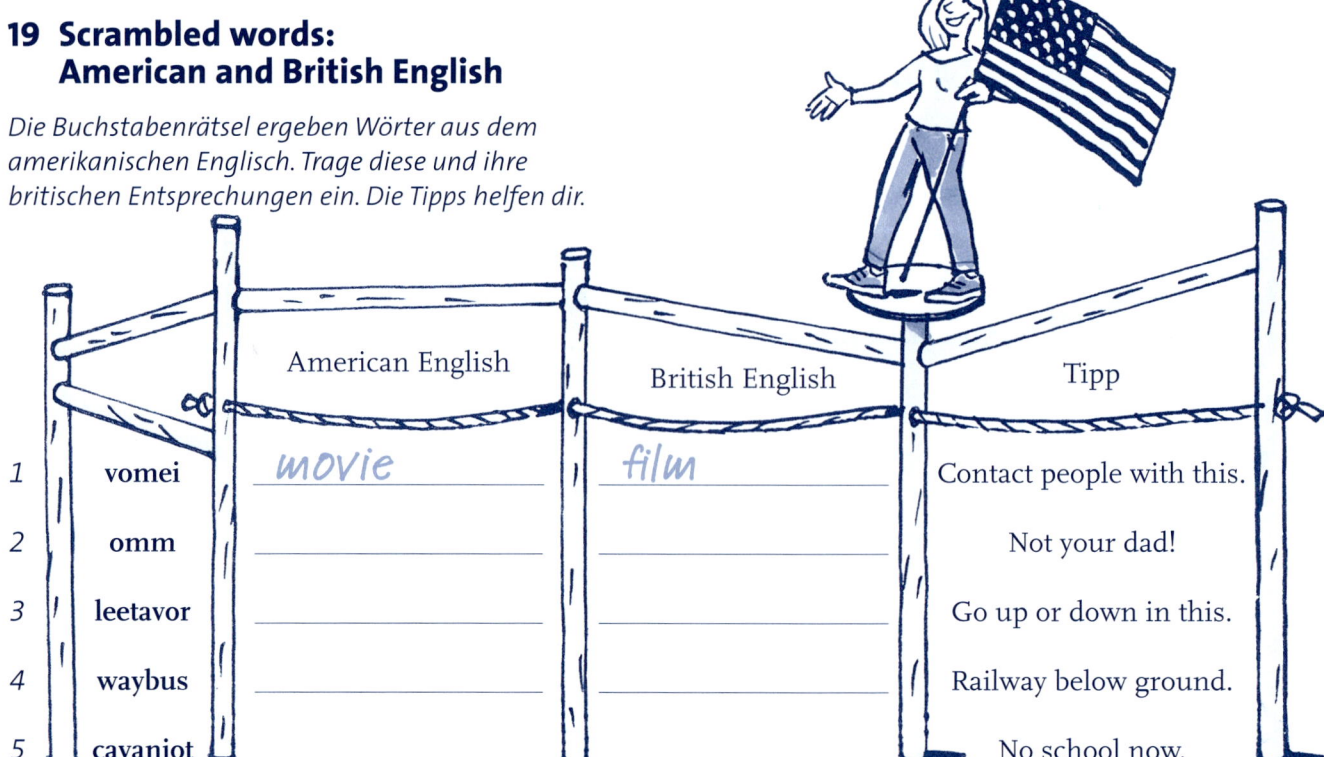

		American English	British English	Tipp
1	vomei	movie	film	Contact people with this.
2	omm			Not your dad!
3	leetavor			Go up or down in this.
4	waybus			Railway below ground.
5	cavaniot			No school now.

18 Crossword

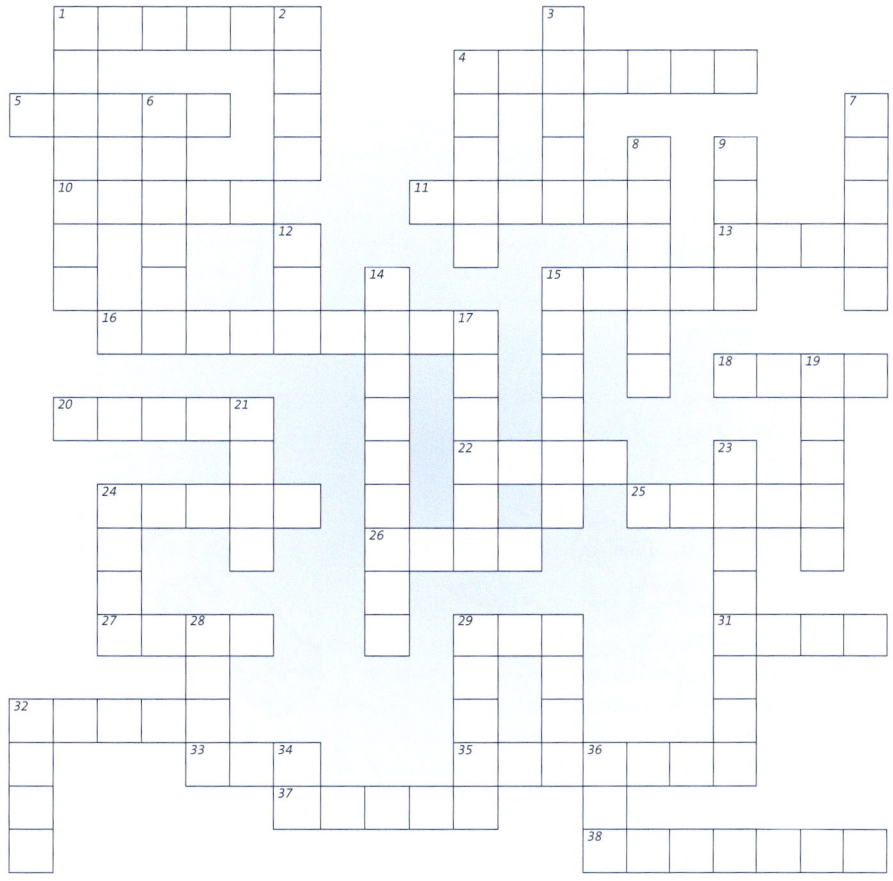

Across ➡

1 A cathedral is a kind of ★. (6)
4 a school subject in which you learn about animals, flowers, etc. (9)
5 You need it to cut bread. (5)
10 opposite of 'late' (5)
11 opposite of 'old-fashioned' (6)
13 a name for the underground in London (4)
15 Somebody stole my bike I was ★ in the shop. (5)
16 In this sport, you run, jump, etc. (9)
19 You need it when you play hockey, tennis, etc. (4)
20 oranges, apples, bananas, etc. (5)
22 60 minutes – an hour / 30 minutes – ★ an hour (4)
24 newspapers, magazines, radio, TV, the Internet, etc. (5)
25 a person who trains a sports team (5)
26 the person at work who tells you what you have to do (4)
27 opposite of 'first' (4)
29 opposite of 'buy'
31 from all ★ England = from every part of England (4)
32 one – once / two – ★ (5)
33 You can do this in the mountains in winter.
35 the most important city in a country (7)
37 not very clever; stupid (5)
38 a building where you can watch a football match (7)

Down ⬇

1 when people play music for an audience (7)
2 very, very big (4)
3 another word for 'film' (5)
4 I like ★ and eggs for breakfast. (5)
6 opposite of 'remember' (6)
7 The wife of a king is a ★ . (5)
8 opposite of 'beginning' (6)
9 another word for 'friend' (4)
12 I'm 14. What ★ are you? (3)
14 This gives you information about when buses, trains, etc. arrive and leave. (9)
15 They're round. A car has got four of them. (6)
17 the things which tourists like to see (6)
19 Can you turn on the ★ ? It's so dark here. (5)
21 one of two children born at the same time
23 city or village – local / country – ★ (8)
24 Breakfast is the first ★ of the day.
28 I see – he ★ (4)
29 opposite of 'mild' (5)
32 make – made / take – ★ (4)
34 they are / she ★ (2)
36 his/hers/ ★ (3)

Lösungen

Introduction

1 Lost words
1 In, 2 of, 3 from, 4 to, 5 at, 6 by,
7 before, 8 between

2 Verb forms
2 show – showed – shown
3 spend – spent – spent
4 hide – hid – hidden
5 do – did – done
6 take – took – taken
7 fly – flew – flown
8 read – read – read
9 throw – threw – thrown
10 speak – spoke – spoken
11 write – wrote – written
12 ride – rode – ridden

3 Crossword

4 Last letter – first letter
1 drum 2 mixture 3 electric 4 concert
5 trumpet 6 trombone 7 enough 8 half
9 fiddle 10 elevator 11 recorder

5 Word search

violin – Violine/Geige,
piano – Klavier, trumpet – Trompete,
drum – Trommel, saxophone – Saxophon
fiddle – Violine/Geige, guitar – Gitarre,
recorder – Blockflöte, flute – Querflöte

6 Word groups
places in town
department store, hospital, hostel, leisure
centre, police station, restaurant
jobs
engineer, fireman, paramedic,
policewoman, teacher, waiter
clothes
dress, jacket, pyjamas, shoes, skirt, trousers
animals
deer, frog, hedgehog, mole, squirrel,
woodpecker

Unit 1

1 Word friends
do: a good job, a project, nothing
listen: carefully, to music, to the teacher
get: angry, dressed, ready
have: a baby, a cold, enough time
look: after the baby, different, for the money

2 Classroom English
1 c, 2 b, 3 a, 4 c

3 Definitions
1 move – four – **wheels**
2 important – country – **capital**
3 places – photos – **sights**
4 woman – king – **queen**
5 big – king – **palace**
6 live – lots – **concert**

4 Spot the mistakes
1 kapital: capital, off: of
2 parlament: parliament, saights: sights
3 tikets: tickets, unterground: underground
4 linie: line, zentral: central
5 chainge: change, Squar: Square

5 Word ladder

save, **have**, **hate**, **date**, **late**, **lane**, **line**,
fine, **mine**, **mile**, milk

6 More about ... London Underground

2 because, 3 only, 4 before, 5 and, 6 ground,
7 too, 8 when, 9 more, 10 Although

7 Crossword: places in a city

¹P	A	L	A	²C	E			³L	
A				A				A	
R			⁴S	T	A	⁵T	I	O	N
K		⁶C	H		O			W	E
		I		E		W			
	⁷B	R	I	D	G	E		⁸S	
		C		R		R		Q	
		U		A				U	
		S	⁹L	I	B	R	A	R	Y
						R			
		¹⁰M	U	S	E	U	M		

8 Hidden words

1 plate, 2 plane, 3 lane, 4 ear, 5 train,
6 arm, 7 planet, 8 mail, 9 late, 10 learn

9 Word families

1 explain, 2 win, 3 smile, 4 fly, 5 act,
6 laugh, 7 build, 8 describe,
9 rehearse, 10 glue, 11 move, 12 explore

10 Word building

1 **dancing lessons** – Tanzstunden
2 **family tree** – Stammbaum
3 **sports centre** – Sportzentrum
4 **sound file** – Tondatei
5 **football boots** – Fußballschuhe
6 **film star** – Filmstar
7 **doorbell** – Türklingel
8 **classroom** – Klassenraum
9 **homework** – Hausaufgabe
10 **wheelchair** – Rollstuhl,
11 **football** – Fußball
12 **weekend** – Wochenende

11 Odd word out

1 adult, 2 budgie, 3 CD-player,
4 trendy, 5 dish, 6 ball

12 The best word

1 angry, 2 shy, 3 proud, 4 puzzled,
5 scared, 6 nervous

13 Word search

Ü	L	F	F	A	H	R	P	L	A	N	S
M	A	L	L	S	Z	X	A	T	B	F	T
S	S	U	U	J	U	A	U	A	A	A	R
T	T	G	G	J	G	B	S	X	H	E	A
E	W	S	Z	B	U	S	S	I	N	H	S
I	A	T	E	A	U	P	T	N	S	R	S
G	G	E	U	U	I	Y	E	C	T	E	E
E	E	I	G	T	C	M	I	C	E	Z	N
N	N	G	R	O	J	B	G	W	I	F	B
F	L	U	G	H	A	F	E	N	G	O	A
C	V	C	Q	B	A	H	N	H	O	F	H
E	F	E	I	N	S	T	E	I	G	E	N

Fahrplan – timetable, **Bus** – bus,
Flughafen – airport, **einsteigen** – get on,
Bahnhof – station, **umsteigen** – change,
Lastwagen – lorry, **Flugsteig** – gate,
Flugzeug – plane, **Auto** – car,
Zug – train, **aussteigen** – get off,
Taxi – taxi, **Bahnsteig** – platform,
Fähre – ferry, **Straßenbahn** – tram

14 The fourth word

1 instrument, 2 queen, 3 south,
4 United Kingdom, 5 central, 6 right,
7 adult, 8 wheels, 9 head, 10 twice

15 Opposites

1 national, 2 spicy, 3 clean, 4 right,
5 loudly, 6 weak, 7 impossible, 8 leave,
9 rich, 10 closed, 11 single, 12 friends,
13 quiet, 14 sad

16 Pronunciation

e – already, bread, breakfast, dead, head, ready
iː – clean, beach, cheap, eastbound, leave, tea
ɪə – dear, clear, disappear, ear, idea, near

17 One or two letters?

fiddle, middle, student, hidden, ready, model
afraid, giraffe, traffic, often, difficult, left
another, beginning, dinner, tunnel, enemy,
pencil, alphabet, always, brilliant, realistic,
alone, pullover

18 Hour glasses

```
1  A S K
2  Y O U T H
3  P A P E R
4  C L E A N
5    A R M
       M
6    C A P
7  D I R T Y
8  C A K E S
9  C H E E R
10   A T E
```

```
1  I C E
2  A B O U T
3  R O M A N
4  H A P P Y
5    B A G
       R
6    B I N
7  E S S A Y
8  T O O T H
9  M O N E Y
10   U S E
```

Das geheime Wort lautet:
Englisch – comparisons
Deutsch – Vergleiche

19 Picture puzzle

a purse, a dice, a pencil sharpener, a pencil,
a helmet, a sandwich, an apple, a fish

Unit 2

1 Word friends

1 eat, 2 wait, 3 catch, 4 read, 5 speak,
6 listen, 7 know, 8 do, 9 become, 10 keep

2 Classroom English

1 b, 2 c, 3 a

3 The fourth word

1 vegetable, 2 stupid, 3 bakery, 4 flight,
5 pork, 6 bottom, 7 forget, 8 teach, 9 wives,
10 farmer

4 Odd word out

1 farm, 2 farmer, 3 danger, 4 bacon,
5 lorry, 6 station, 7 three, 8 first, 9 wait,
10 mate, 11 oil rig, 12 button

5 Words with different meanings

1 **single** – ledig/einfache
2 **change** – Wechselgeld/umsteigen
3 **timetable** – Fahrplan/Stundenplan
4 **spend** – ausgeben/verbringen
5 **rock** – Rock/Fels
6 **walk** – zu Fuß gehen/Spaziergang

6 Last letter – first letter

1 timetable, 2 excited, 3 departure,
4 elephant, 5 take, 6 elevator,
7 rock, 8 key, 9 you,
10 until, 11 luckily, 12 yet

7 Word groups

farm animals
chicken, sheep, lamb, horse, cow, turkey
media
mobile, television, radio, sound file, magazine, newspaper
transport
arrival, departure, timetable, Tube, bus stop,
station

8 Spot the mistakes

1 biger: bigger, ilands: islands
2 kieps: keeps, werld: world
3 have: has, mobil: mobile
4 write: writes, weak: week
5 musik: music, webseite: website
6 taked: took, fotos: photos

9 Number crossword

```
R I N G T O N E       M
O               N       A
C           C O A S T
K     H U G E   R       E
      N         R
      T   T W I C E
M E D I A       V
I     L         A
X         O I L
```

10 Word pairs

catch – ball, **do** – course, **download** – sound file,
pack – rucksack, **play** – recorder,
read – menu, **send** – message, **wear** – helmet

11 Scrambled words: school

1 **timetable** – Stundenplan
2 **teacher** – Lehrer,
3 **classmate** – Klassenkamerad/in,
4 **holidays** – (Schul-)Ferien,
5 **board** – Tafel,
6 **science** – Naturwissenschaft,
7 **classroom** – Klassenraum

12 The best word

1 exciting, 2 funny, 3 upset, 4 huge,
5 realistic

13 Making phrases

1 take, *2* send, *3* check, *4* feed, *5* get off,
6 phone

14 Word search: town and country words

O	I	A	J	F	I	E	L	D	S	F	K
S	G	R	O	A	D	B	U	I	T	X	B
Q	L	F	F	H	A	R	B	O	U	R	R
U	A	A	M	O	U	N	T	A	I	N	I
A	K	R	K	V	G	U	S	Y	Z	T	D
R	E	M	H	I	L	L	M	C	I	O	G
E	S	O	B	B	J	P	Y	A	S	W	E
O	E	S	T	A	T	I	O	N	L	E	S
C	A	S	T	L	E	E	M	A	A	R	K
B	B	E	A	C	H	V	V	L	N	Q	N
D	A	X	C	O	A	S	T	O	D	X	O
C	T	H	R	I	V	E	R	Q	I	B	Q

field – Feld/Sportplatz, **road** – Straße,
harbour – Hafen, **mountain** – Berg,
hill – Hügel, **station** – Bahnhof,
castle – Schloss, **beach** – Strand,
coast – Küste, **river** – Fluss,
square – Platz, **lake** – See,
sea – Meer, **farm** – Bauernhof,
island – Insel, **canal** – Kanal,
tower – Turm, **bridge** – Brücke

15 More about … Orkney

1 islands *2* on, *3* biggest, *4* and, *5* but,
6 under, *7* another, *8* between, *9* takes,
10 for, *11* make, *12* history

16 Lost words

1 unsafe, *2* healthy, *3* untidy,
4 unhealthy, *5* happy, *6* unfriendly,
7 right, *8* upset, *9* sorry

17 Opposites

1 interesting, *2* old, *3* unhappy/sad, *4* right,
5 winter, *6* over, *7* outside, *8* evening,
9 hate, *10* unfriendly, *11* nobody, *12* answer

18 Vocabulary network

SCHOOL
do: a test, a project on Scotland, homework
work: alone, in a small group, with a partner
listen to: the CD, an explanation, a recording
SPORTS
play: football, hockey, tennis
go: swimming, riding, surfing
do: judo, sport, yoga
HOBBIES AND FREE TIME
play: the drums, the piano, the trumpet
collect: model cars, postcards, stamps
visit: a friend, grandma, museums

Unit 3

1 Words in pictures

a) *1* face, *2* eye, *3* nose, *4* ear, *5* teeth,
    6 hair, *7* mouth, *8* finger, *9* hand
b) *1* pretty/round, *2* blue/bright,
    3 long/small, *4* my left/right,
    5 broken/white, *6* grey/tidy,
    7 a big/loud, *8* clean/strong

2 Hidden words

1 nose, *2* singer, *3* east, *4* sea, *5* stone,
6 train, *7* star, *8* rain, *9* orange, *10* great,
11 art

3 Word families

a) *2* listen, *3* explain, *4* explore,
    5 play, *6* mix, *7* move, *8* paint,
    9 phone, *10* practise, *11* describe,
    12 invite, *13* teach, *14* translate
b) *1* meaning – explain
    2 invitation – invite
    3 practise
    4 phone – arrive
    5 translation

4 Word friends

enter: a building, a room, a shop
score: again, three goals, a point
spot: a mistake, a fire, a hair in the soup
lock: the car, the suitcase, the window
train: at a sports club, hard, twice a week

5 Classroom English

1 c, *2* a, *3* b

6 Definitions

1 place – ship: **quay**
2 looks – person: **clone**
3 team – matches: **supporter**
4 last – winner: **final**
5 hotel – eat: **hostel**
6 most – school: **head teacher**

7 Word ladder

need – **feed** – **feet** – **meet** – **meat** – **beat** – **boat** – **boot** – **book** – **took** – **cook** – **look** – **lock** – luck

8 What are the words?

1 information – is, 2 homework was,
3 is – hair, 4 transport – isn't, 5 is – news

9 Pronunciation

ə – colour, famous, harbour, nervous
aʊ – around, cloud, house, proud
uː – group, soup, through, you
ʌ – cousin, double, enough, touch
ɔː – bought, course, yours, thought

10 Crossword

swimming trunks und *first half* werden auseinander geschrieben.

11 More about … Manchester United

1 club, 2 times, 3 third, 4 over, 5 millions,
6 rich, 7 players, 8 huge, 9 match, 10 even,
11 than, 12 learn

12 Last letter – first letter

1 stress, 2 subject, 3 train, 4 news, 5 shirt,
6 travel, 7 lessons, 8 show, 9 words,
10 ship, 11 papers, 12 stadium, 13 meaning,
14 goalkeeper, 15 realistic

13 Hour glasses

Das geheime Wort lautet:
Englisch – goalkeepers,
Deutsch – Torwarte/Torfrauen

14 Word search

room
bed, chair, cupboard, lamp, shelf, sofa, table, wardrobe
clothes
anorak, pullover, shoe, shorts, skirt, sock, trainers, trousers
transport
bus, ferry, lorry, plane, ship, taxi, tram, underground
sport
athletics, cup, goal, medal, Paralympics, skis, stadium, volleyball
food
chips, hamburger, pizza, pork, salad, sausage, soup, spaghetti

Unit 4

1 Classroom English
1 a, *2* c, *3* b, *4* c

2 School words
1 board, *2* choir, *3* class, *4* students,
5 history, *6* biology, *7* pencil, *8* teacher,
9 art, *10* essay
Das geheime Wort lautet:
Englisch – dictionary, Deutsch – Wörterbuch

3 Word pairs
build – stadium, **call** – ambulance,
climb – mountain, **cook** – meal,
correct – mistake, **grow** – lettuce,
listen to – live music, **read** – magazine,
score – goal, **turn on** – light,
wear – football shirt, **win** – medal

4 One or two letters?
reggae, beginning, language, baggy, fog,
foggy
collect, adult, until, medal, model,
pullover
community, swimmer, woman, grammar,
moment, thermometer
report, shopping, unhappy, appetite,
represent, disappear
diary, married, guitar, tired, hurry,
different
promise, essay, glasses, guess, husband,
island
bottle, water, pretty, weather, spaghetti

5 Vocabulary network
TRAVEL
visit: a castle, an old church, a museum
pack: a suitcase, a bag, a rucksack
go: by train, on holiday, on a boat trip
SPORT AND FREE TIME
win: a cup, a medal, a prize
go: canoeing, fishing, snowshoeing
wear: running shoes, a helmet, pads
NOT WELL
feel: terrible, ill, weak
have: a sore throat, a cold, a temperature
phone: an ambulance, a doctor, the hospital

6 Verb forms
2 beat – beat – beaten
3 break – broke – broken
4 cut – cut – cut
5 draw – drew – drawn
6 fight – fought – fought
7 find – found – found
8 grow – grew – grown
9 forget – forgot – forgotten
10 let – let – let
11 mean – meant – meant
12 upset – upset – upset

7 Spot the mistakes
1 childs: children, beers: bears
2 realy: really, off: of
3 allso: also, danger: dangerous
4 usualy: usually, errly: early
5 ran: run, swimers: swimmers
6 interresting: interesting, catchs: catches
7 stand: stands, quitely: quietly
8 bare: bear, jump: jumps

8 Word search

L	S	J	E	C	G	H	E	D	G	E	H	O	G	C
I	Q	F	L	H	I	O	V	X	R	S	N	A	K	E
O	U	O	E	I	R	M	H	M	H	T	M	N	X	S
N	I	X	P	C	A	O	O	A	I	S	B	H	R	C
S	R	F	H	K	F	U	R	I	N	E	S	C	O	F
H	R	X	A	E	F	S	S	M	O	N	K	E	Y	Y
E	E	Z	N	N	E	E	E	C	Y	W	A	E	S	U
E	L	K	T	P	I	G	K	K	Z	I	N	H	F	G
P	F	F	S	B	O	B	C	Y	A	B	G	A	I	B
Q	R	T	N	Y	S	E	S	L	D	P	A	M	S	U
Y	O	U	G	F	X	A	M	O	L	E	R	S	H	D
P	G	R	C	O	W	R	P	A	R	R	O	T	N	G
V	Z	K	G	O	F	P	H	I	P	P	O	E	K	I
K	X	E	C	R	O	C	O	D	I	L	E	R	W	E
X	H	Y	G	R	A	B	B	I	T	I	G	E	R	Y

10 Lost words
1 at, *2* against, *3* on, *4* until, *5* inside,
6 near, *7* about, *8* onto, *9* off, *10* in

11 Odd word out
1 minute, *2* chorus, *3* per cent, *4* shoe,
5 build, *6* sledges, *7* gig, *8* coast

12 The fourth word
1 kilometre, *2* player, *3* themselves, *4* number,
5 instrument, *6* year, *7* moon, *8* women

13 More about ... traditional Inuit hunting
1 temperatures, *2* much, *3* fishing, *4* land,
5 just, *6* kind, *7* used, *8* could, *9* built,
10 cold

14 Number crossword

Crossword grid:

Across and down answers filled in:
- R, P
- KNIFE, SMOKE
- L (LATEST), DIALOGUE
- ESCAPE, CHORUS
- ADULT, LEADER
- WE (WEIGHT), CABIN
- STRIKE

(Grid letters: 1 R, 2 P, 3 KNIFE, 4 SMOKE, 5 L, 6 DIALOGUE, 7 ESCAPE, 8 A, 9 CHORUS, 10 S, 11 A, 12 ADULT, 13 LEADER, 14 WE, 15 C CABIN, 16 STRIKE)

15 Word groups

jobs:
actor, cleaner, engineer, painter, shop assistant, waiter

music:
band, choir, chorus, instrument, concert, song

station:
departure, railway, suitcases, ticket machines, timetable, toilets, trains

weather:
cloudy, fog, rain, snow, stormy, sunny, tornado

16 Opposites

1 untidy, 2 cheap, 3 modern, 4 off, 5 under, 6 leave, 7 bottom, 8 remember, 9 departures, 10 wife, 11 boring, 12 cold, 13 dirty, 14 upstairs

Unit 5

1 Word families

1 draw, 2 revise, 3 spell, 4 draw, 5 explain, 6 live, 7 attack, 8 support, 9 mean, 10 laugh

2 The best word

1 final, 2 strict, 3 artificial, 4 silly

3 Last letter – first letter

1 chorus, 2 stomach, 3 hunt, 4 twins, 5 strict, 6 trousers, 7 spelling 8 grandma, 9 audience, 10 editor, 11 revise, 12 electric, 13 curry, 14 yes, 15 section

4 The fourth word

1 vegetable, 2 dish, 3 country, 4 month, 5 instrument, 6 planet, 7 colour, 8 art

5 Pronunciation

ʊ – bully, full, pull, put, push, sugar

juː – computer, community, excuse, huge, menu, tube

ʌ – but, fun, publish, summer, trumpet, tunnel

6 Word building

1 text message: SMS
2 car park: Parkplatz
3 chat room: Chatroom
4 running shoes: Laufschuhe, Sportschuhe
5 rock music: Rockmusik
6 semi-final: Halbfinale
7 north-east: Nordosten, nordöstlich
8 bedroom: Schlafzimmer
9 snowshoes: Schneeschuhe
10 classmate: Klassenkamerad/in

7 Making phrases

1 turn, 2 tidy, 3 revise, 4 talk, 5 grow, 6 look, 7 escape, 8 agree

7 Hour glasses

Left grid:
1 SPY
2 SMOKE
3 BULLY
4 WHILE
5 ICE
E
6 OWN
7 SHOOT
8 LAMBS
9 STAGE
10 END

Right grid:
1 ACT
2 SHEEP
3 CANOE
4 METRE
5 GIG
M
6 SEX
7 WATCH
8 LORRY
9 GUESS
10 ASK

Das geheime Wort lautet:
Englisch – centimetres, Deutsch Zentimeter

8 Word ladder

film – **file – fine – line – mine – mile – male – mole – hole – role –rule – rude – ride – hide – side** – size

9 Word search - The media

magazine – Zeitschrift
record – aufnehmen/Schallplatte
radio – Radio
news – Nachrichten
television – Fernsehen
editor – Redakteur/in
book – Buch
programme – Programm
report – Bericht
article – Artikel
newspaper – Zeitung
mail – E-Mail/mailen
publish – veröffentlichen
mobile – Handy/Mobiltelefon

10 Classroom English

1 c, *2* a, *3* a, *4* b

11 Words in pictures: fruit and vegetables

1 bright, red, tomatoes
2 delicious, forest, mushrooms
3 sweet, Spanish, oranges
4 hard, green, apples
5 big, garden, onions
6 delicious, German, strawberries
7 bright, orange, carrots
8 healthy, green, lettuce
9 delicious, new, potatoes
10 long, yellow, bananas

12 Opposites

1 worst, *2* bad, *3* top, *4* dark, *5* unhealthy,
6 old-fashioned, *7* late, *8* untidy, *9* behind,
10 answer, *11* take ... off, *12* arrival, *13* right,
14 forget

13 Words with different meanings

1 **revise** – wiederholen/überarbeiten
2 **cross** – überqueren/sauer
3 **train** – Zug/trainieren,
4 **about** – über/ungefähr,
5 **save** – retten/sparen,
6 **final** – Endspiel/letzte,
7 **stomach** – Bauch/Magen

14 Definitions

1 important – team: captain
2 work – more: strike
3 spend – home: sleepover
4 corrects – texts: editor
5 picture – pen: drawing
6 word – holidays: vacation

15 Hidden words

1 cinema, *2* listen, *3* tram, *4* castle *5* scan,
6 tunnel, *7* uncle, *8* mice, *9* sister,
10 summer/autumn, *11* clean

16 Word ladder

film – file – fine – line – mine – mile – male –
mole – role – rule – rude – ride – hide – side –
size

17 Word friends

1 revise, *2* produce, *3* make, *4* record, *5* play,
6 go, *7* be, *8* have, *9* laugh, *10* skim,
11 keep, *12* remember

18 Odd word out

1 picture, *2* publish, *3* section, *4* draw,
5 score, *6* career, *7* captain, *8* popular,
9 drawing, *10* movie

19 Scrambled words: American and British English

1 movie, film, *2* mom, mum, *3* elevator, lift,
4 subway, underground, *5* vacation, holidays

20 Crossword

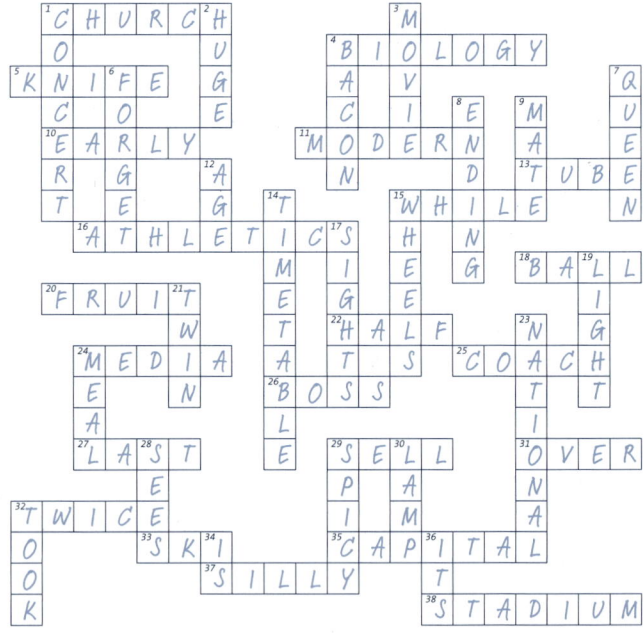